SELF-PUBLISHING WITH AMAZON ADS

THE AUTHOR'S GUIDE TO LOWER COSTS, HIGHER ROYALTIES, AND GREATER PEACE OF MIND

BRYAN COHEN

INTRODUCTION
HOW DO AMAZON ADS WORK?

"So, what's your trick?" The author asked, staring directly into her laptop camera.

I paused for a moment as I let the words sink into our Zoom call.

"I'm not sure exactly what you mean," I said, a bit worried about where this would take our coaching call.

"You know, what's your gimmick? Pardon my frankness, but what's your tease that gets me all excited about shiny, new Amazon ads and makes me want to study with the 'so-called master' of Amazon advertising?" she asked with a grin. "What's your trick?"

I took a second to compose my words. Most of my sessions on book marketing didn't quite head in this direction. But Erin was a trailblazer.

"I've found that Amazon ads are trick-free, in a way," I said. "They're more likely to work for you if you use them wisely, but they won't make you rich overnight."

Erin seemed to anticipate my answer.

"Then why all the bells and whistles? I know we all need to make a living, but why the challenges and the course?" she asked. "If this isn't some flashy gimmick, then what is it?"

"Amazon ads can help any author grow with incremental improvements. And those small changes make big opportunities for the future," I said. "It takes time, it's methodical, and the numbers may not be huge, but it's 100% achievable."

Erin seemed to trust me about as far as she could throw me.

"Well, I'm not completely buying it, Guru," she said. "But you've got my attention."

"Good! I'll take that to start," I said. "But right now, let me begin by explaining how Amazon ads work."

* * *

I'm Bryan Cohen; an author, a teacher, and an advertiser. I've been fortunate enough to have self-published my own books for the past 11 years. During that time, I've seen a lot of marketing methods come and go. I've tried pretty much everything under the sun, and many didn't work as well as I'd hoped.

But in 2016, I began experimenting with Amazon ads for both my fiction and my nonfiction books. Through trial, error, and a lot of coffee, I found that certain aspects of this marketing platform weren't exactly beginner friendly. But since I could see great promise with ads that actually showed up where your self-published books are sold, I took on the task of learning the platform so I could teach it. I knew that if I could help authors like you get over a few initial hurdles, Amazon ads could be the starter marketing plan for 99% of the author community.

Fast forward half a decade, and I've had the good fortune of helping over 30,000 authors work with ads. Some of those authors have had life-changing results with significantly higher profits. From the full-time Zamboni driver and parent to two who was able to quit to focus on writing, to the grandmother and caretaker who hadn't seen a profit in nine years reaching $1,000 in royalties a month, we've seen hundreds of success stories from using Amazon Ads.

We've proudly helped dozens of authors reach $5,000 a month in royalties while assisting ten publishing powerhouses to reach the hallowed $10,000 per month mark. We'll share some of their profitable journeys later in the book.

And though there are authors who don't find these ads a good fit for them, thousands of others have found the platform an encouraging way to take back control of their author careers.

As you saw, this introduction began with a story. Throughout this book, we'll alternate between a narrative where I coach an author, named Erin, toward success with her books. In between these parts of my little tale, I will share the nuts and bolts of Amazon ads. I'm hoping this will help you learn more than just the step one, step two, and step three of this platform. My goal is to show you both the outer and the inner game of book marketing using the Amazon ads platform.

How do Amazon ads work? They start with a commitment. They continue with a bird's eye view of your royalties. They can be sustained with consistency, and they can grow by trusting the numbers. I've seen too many authors falter in one of those four key areas. I've also seen plenty of authors read every book under the sun about book marketing, without giving one of them a full 100% shot at success. My hope is that you'll read this book, and that you'll do the exercises to give yourself the best chance of success.

Before we get to the good stuff, I want to mention that this book was funded and supported by the self-publishing author community. After generous contributions from over 600 authors, this book sprung to life as part of a November 2021 Kickstarter campaign. Thank you to everyone who helped to make this book possible, and thank you to you, reader, for ordering this book, and for taking control of your book marketing journey.

* * *

Erin sighed. "Are you going to stop with the woo-woo already, and tell me what I'm supposed to do to make more money on my books?"

"All I'm trying to do is make sure you're really understanding that patience part," I said.

"Enough with the teaching. Enough with the philosophizing. Let's just get to the good stuff."

CHAPTER 1

WHY IS IT WORTH TRYING ONE MORE BOOK MARKETING THING?

I took a deep breath as I looked at the clock. It was just a few more minutes until the start of my first call with Erin, the lucky winner in a recent contest I'd run for authors.

She'd been publishing for about five years and had tried her hand at three genres: sci-fi, nonfiction, and small-town romance. In her entry, she'd mentioned the familiar refrain that she'd tried to make ads work for her, but they never seemed to stick. She asked if she had any chance of making this work or if she should just ditch the profession entirely. With her name being randomly drawn from over a thousand entries, it was my mission over months-worth of coaching sessions to help her never think about quitting again.

Following her victory, I'd gotten a bit of an aloof vibe from the emails we'd exchanged. But I figured that as soon as we hopped on a call together, things would go incredibly smooth. After a few minutes of small talk, that wasn't exactly how it went down.

"I've tried everything, Bryan. I've tried it all and none of it seems to work," she said. "I've done Facebook ads, email list building, TikTok, and of course, your precious Amazon ads."

I couldn't help but laugh at that last bit. "They aren't just my Amazon ads," I said. "There's plenty enough to go around for everyone. But I do appreciate your honesty. Please, don't hold back on telling me how you really feel."

Erin held her breath for a moment. "Are you absolutely sure about that?" she asked. "You seem like a nice guy and I don't want to hurt your feelings."

"I think the only way this coaching thing works is if you lay all your cards on the table," I said. "I've been on stages, in front of crowds, and even on a game show. I'm sure you won't rattle me too much."

"Fair enough. Because you asked, I won't hold anything back," she said. "Look, I appreciate you giving me this contest win. I know some people think you're like this big ad guru or something."

"There are plenty of people who think the exact opposite," I said.

She cringed. "And in all honesty, I might be one of them."

Cue the butterflies in my stomach. Maybe she could rattle me after all. I wasn't sure exactly how to reply, and Erin snatched away the silence.

"So, all-wise Guru, tell it to me straight. Why on earth should I try one more marketing thing when nothing else has worked to this point?"

I tried to suppress my worries. After all, if Erin won this huge prize but she didn't have much faith in me, how would I help her succeed?

I cleared my throat. "You don't have to do anything you don't want to do," I said. "You can choose to keep publishing, put out your books, and hope for the best."

"I don't think you made this whole hullabaloo about my 'high-value' prize to just tell me to write more books," she said with a grin.

"Don't worry," I said. "There's an 'or.' Or, instead of hoping your books stand out on their own with random people crashing into them, you can try a method that sends you new readers, and that thousands of authors have used to find more success."

Erin shook her head in my general direction. "I really do want to believe, honestly, but I don't want to lose money doing these ads. I don't want them to take me away from my writing. I don't want it to take me two bucks to get a dollar back in sales," she said. "How are Amazon ads any different from all the rest of the tricks out there?"

* * *

I totally understood where Erin was coming from with her skepticism. A lot of authors trying Amazon ads for the first time have been burned before. They've heard that something was incredibly easy, or incredibly fast, only to find out that neither of those things were true.

After publishing my first book in 2010 and starting my book marketing podcast, *The Sell More Books Show,* in 2014, I've seen plenty of marketing trends come and go. At the beginning, we were all throwing anything we could against the wall to see if it would stick. Most of it slid down the wall and landed against the floor with a wet *thud.*

But when I tried my hand at Amazon ads, before there were any courses or hubbub, I could feel that something was different about the platform. Once you got past the terminology and the technology, the ads seemed repeatable and consistent. As opposed to one-and-done techniques and more occasional promotions, Amazon ads had a low-heat simmer effect that I really appreciated.

Plenty of strategies have fallen away in the last few years, but the ads have stood the test of time for authors with the patience and prudence to make them work.

Here are a few of the reasons why I think Amazon ads have the capability of being different from some of the things you may have tried before:

1. There is Less Friction

There are plenty of ways to send a reader to a book. Different advertising methods, different email services, different social media platforms. But at any given point, if you have to get someone away from what they are currently doing to head over to Amazon to buy your book, it will take extra effort.

Some readers might not want to jump off Facebook or TikTok to go buy something. Some readers are just trying to get to "inbox is zero," (a Herculean task, for sure) and your promo email doesn't stir their soul. But if you run an ad through Amazon Advertising, where readers are already looking for a book to buy, then they don't have to make as much of an effort. They're already on Amazon, so they don't have to think twice about staying on the site. It's like having to get up out of your comfy loveseat and grab a drink from the fridge. It's a pain to do it, but it's a whole lot easier if there's a mini-fridge just to your left. Amazon ads can be the convenient mini-fridge for reaching new readers.

2. With the Right Settings, These Ads Are Cheaper

They say that the hardest dollar to earn in an online business is your first. Once you figure out how to make a buck, it becomes easier to make two, and then three, and then ten, and so on. This means that at first you may not be profitable, but eventually, with enough practice and education, you can get to the point where you earn $1, and $2, and more.

In the pursuit of making this self-publishing journey successful for you, we want to spend as little money as possible. All of us lose a little money to begin with, that's the cost of education in self-publishing. But if you could choose to sacrifice less money upfront to get those initial results, that seems like a pretty good deal, right?

With Amazon ads, you can usually get potential readers to click your ad for $0.39 or lower. To get someone who might be interested in your book to be just one click away from making that purchase, you can do it for less than a full-size Snickers in a vending machine. It's relatively cheap, as far as book marketing goes, and while things may change to a certain extent in the future, as of the writing of this book, paying for a click with Amazon ads is one of the best deals in self-publishing.

3. Amazon Ads Can Multiply Your Marketing

I was speaking with a student of my Author Ad School course the other day, James Dillehay, and he listed out half a dozen ways that his ads had led to additional benefits for his books. By sending more traffic (a.k.a. readers) to his books, he had shown Amazon that when readers actually find his title, they are pretty likely to buy. This led to Amazon sending additional traffic, through search and its automated email, to his titles. This led to even more sales of his books in addition to sales he got directly from his ads. Through his ads and the eventual organic sales from his long-term advertising, James reached over $10,000 a month in royalties from his books.

Wouldn't it be nice if Amazon simply started sending more people over to your books for free? In James' case, it took multiple months of advertising to get to this point, so it wasn't really free, but it made the affordable deal we talked about earlier even better.

Amazon ads also tend to get a boost when you have additional traffic, like a $0.99 discount promotion. We'll get into this as a specific advertising strategy a little bit later, but it's helpful to know that when you run ads and something else good happens to your book, (like a viral TikTok or a mention on a podcast), it may help you get even more attention and sales for your book.

Now, it's important to note that when you are trying to focus on running Amazon ads for your books, it's very helpful to get clean data from your efforts. What is clean data? It means you aren't running ads on six different platforms at the same time. I know it's tough to focus on only one thing at a time, but it'll be difficult to tell if your ads are helping your book to profit if you have way too much noise going on in your book marketing life. It can be extremely helpful to establish an entire month where the only paid promo you run is an Amazon ad to get the cleanest possible data.

If your books are significantly profitable, I certainly wouldn't turn any other ads off, but if you're losing money or breaking even, it might be worth trying to go Amazon ads solo for a while.

I've got a few exercises for you to try before we move into the meat and potatoes. You are a lot more likely to get results from this book if you work on these tasks while you're reading.

* * *

Chapter 1 Exercises

1. Open a new document on your computer and name it *Self-Publishing with Amazon Ads Notes.*

2. Flip back through this chapter and write down which of the three reasons I shared, about Amazon ads being a successful next step, spoke to you the most. Write this down in your notes document.

3. Write down on a scale of one to ten, how positive are you feeling about Amazon ads and their chance to help your profitability?

* * *

"How am I feeling about my chances with ads?" Erin asked. "And we're still doing the honesty thing, right?"

I took a deep breath. "I think I can handle the truth," I said.

"Whatever you say. Let me know if you need a break from it," she said. "I'm about a three right now."

"At least that's better than a one?" I asked.

"I don't know," she said. "Maybe I'm just not a good fit for this. I need something to work. I really do need it."

Erin seemed to have a weird reaction when she said the word "Need." This almost imperceptible twitch stuck out to me, and I decided to keep it in mind for later sessions.

She continued. "And even though I need it, maybe another author would be a better fit," she said. "I have a few friends—"

"No take backs," I said. "Besides, you're already here. You still haven't even done the first homework yet. Given that I've seen Amazon ads help a lot of people figure out why their books weren't selling, isn't it worth the chance that you might join their ranks?"

Erin nodded. "It is. I really hope that it is," she said. "I will try my best to do your homework." Something seemed to catch Erin's eye off-camera. "Sorry, family calls. You handled the truth pretty well, Guru. I'll see you at the next call."

Before I could remind Erin there were five minutes left in our session, she abruptly hung up, and left me sitting there with my own thoughts. I sighed into the silence.

This one might take a little extra work.

CHAPTER 2

WHAT KIND OF TIME DO I NEED TO INVEST IN AMAZON ADS?

To make sure I understood my student better ahead of our next meeting, I did a little bit of digging. I scrolled through some of her social media, read a few blog posts, and did a bit of googling.

Through my research, I learned that Erin was a proud mom of three. And while she'd left the working world when her second child was born, she'd gotten the itch to put her stories out into the world when her kids were all school-age. Between a few chapters of her latest book and her public posts, I could tell the take-no-crap mindset was not reserved for me alone.

Now, I had to find a way to cut through her natural skepticism long enough for her to set up her ads.

"I've had a thought about your suggestions with my Amazon ad campaigns," Erin said. I detected her emphasis on the word *suggestions*.

"I'm listening."

"I have my concerns about how long this will take. I know your philosophy on this is supposed to be all nice and cheery and slow as molasses, but how about I just set up three ads max with a $1 bid and see what happens?"

I considered my next words carefully. I knew I had to find a way to get through to her. It was sure to be a challenge. But as many people in the author community know, I love a good challenge.

"I've got a question for you. What are your expectations of how a successful Amazon ad is supposed to look? And how long do you think it's going to take?"

Erin studied me for a moment before she responded. "I guess I expect to know right away if a certain ad is working. I'm not going to sugar coat this. I want to put as little time as possible into this because I'm completely overwhelmed. I have way too much on my plate to think about these ads."

In my experience, Erin was absolutely in the majority with her opinion. If an author didn't know whether the ad was successful in a matter of hours, then they'd consider shutting it off and moving on with their life.

"I really understand that feeling. Between writing the books, getting them edited, publishing them," I said, "there's way too much to keep in your brain at once. It's not fair, but any kind of book marketing, in particular Amazon ads, aren't necessarily going to go the way you expect." I leaned in a little bit. "As much as it's a pain, we can't force them to do anything."

"Fine, fine," she said. "I'll just sacrifice some of my time this week, make 50 ads and then see how they're doing next month when I have more space."

I held my breath for a moment as I attempted to thread the needle. "I'm really glad you're up for making more than a few ads, but these ads aren't exactly the 'set it and forget it' type."

"Well, Guru, I've seen your army of minions responding to your emails, but it's just me over here." She paused. "I'm sorry. It's been a rough week. I just want to know how I'd find the extra time to stare at my ad dashboard every five minutes?"

I knew Erin wasn't alone in this situation, either. I couldn't help but remember the days when I did temp work, freelancing, and book marketing all at the same time to make ends meet.

"It's not going to be every five minutes. But you can't leave the ads to their own devices either. Look, you have kids, right?"

"As far as I know, I have three," she said.

"What would happen if you left them alone in the house for a week, completely to their own devices?"

A smile almost formed on her lips. "I don't think I'd have a house to come back to."

"When you're making and running ads, you need to babysit them a little bit. You create them, you keep an eye on them, and you keep working to get more of them."

I hoped that the regular schedule of Amazon ads wouldn't be a deal breaker. As much as I knew that good things took time to work, I wasn't always the biggest fan of patience myself.

"I catch your drift, but I'm not exactly what I would call excited," she said. "However, I have a feeling you're not just blowing smoke here. So, how much time are we talking about?"

I tried to hide it, but I breathed a sigh of relief. Maybe, just maybe, I was starting to get somewhere with my contest winner. "Just like everything else, it'll take more time than you'd like, but it doesn't have to consume your whole life."

* * *

There's no such thing as a push-button book marketing method. And yet, I see authors using copious amounts of time and energy to hunt down an incredible technique that will let them earn royalties while focusing entirely on the writing. But rather than spending hours each month looking for the Holy Grail, you could consistently work toward sending a steady flow of traffic to your books. With more readers seeing your book each month, you'll regularly get more reliable sales and predictable royalties.

Whenever you start something new or try an ad platform a different way, there will be moments where you feel like you're moving in molasses. Everyone is slow when they're learning a new tactic, but I want to encourage you to stay the course. With practice, you'll get faster, as long as you stick around long enough to get the hang of things.

Now, it can be a little scary to make room on your schedule for book marketing, but the authors who are able to work it in have a much better chance of consistently sending new readers to their books. Let's talk a little bit about what kind of time commitment it takes to give your Amazon ads a better chance to succeed. Here are the three main tasks you need to fit in when you run ads:

1. Researching Targets for Your Ads

There are three main ad types that we like to recommend author advertisers use when they're first starting out. One ad type, Sponsored Product Auto ads, allow Amazon to choose your targets for you. That sounds simple enough.

Another type is the Sponsored Product Category ad. For those ads, you pick a genre or sub-genre that you'd like to target on the platform. We recommend only going with the most relevant categories (a.k.a. similar) to your book. This means after you find five to ten of these or fewer, you won't need to hunt down targets anymore. Easy peasy.

But the last type of ad that we recommend, the Sponsored Product Keyword ad, will require that you go out and look for new keywords on a regular basis. Now, it's important to note that a keyword doesn't just have to be one word. It can be a string of words. Our goal is to find the sort of words that a reader looking for a book on Amazon would use to find a book like yours. This could mean using search terms, like what kind of genre your book is or the types of tropes you might find within. It could be an author who writes in your genre, their book title, or their series name. Pretty much anything can be a keyword phrase.

It's a good idea to learn this process manually at first. But once you do, you can branch off into some free and paid keyword research tools to help you in your process. Some of our favorite tools include Instant

Data Scraper, Also Boughts Downloader by Kindletrends and Publisher Rocket. It's important to note that about half of the work you do on keyword research will actually be editing the lists that you create to get rid of any words that don't actually fit with your book.

We know it sounds daunting and like it requires a huge time commitment from you. The good news is, we recommend setting aside only 30 to 60 minutes a week for keyword research. You can break that into smaller blocks of time to make it more manageable for your busy schedule. That way, it's not as overwhelming as doing it all at once.

2. Creating New Ads

As we mentioned in the previous section, the first two ad types, Sponsored Product Auto and Sponsored Product Category, don't require that you create too many of them. For each book that you plan to run ads on, you might have one auto ad for each format of your book (e-book, paperback, hard cover, et cetera). And for each book that you run ads to, you might have 5 to 10 Sponsored Product Category ads with one category in each ad per format.

But when it comes to keyword ads, we recommend creating five to ten ads per week, focusing mostly on keyword ads for your most profitable book. You can use about 100 to 150 keywords for each of the keyword ads you gather during your weekly research session. It takes a little bit of time to get used to making the ads at first, but all new things take extra time in the beginning until you get the hang of them.

At first, it may take you longer than 30 to 60 minutes a week to create these keyword ads. But after a few weeks of practice, we have found that most authors are able to make these five to ten ads using keywords from their research session in about the same amount of time.

My team and I cover this topic more extensively in our free 5-Day Author Ad Profit Challenge with video walkthroughs and lots of live support. Go to AuthorsAdvertise.com and register to join our next Challenge. Total time commitment: 30 to 60 minutes per week.

3. Analyzing the Numbers

Here's the great news about data analysis. In the beginning, there's not much to do. 70% to 80% of your ads may take 3 to 4 weeks to do anything. While this may be frustrating for some, we think of this as an opportunity. You can focus your efforts on ad creation while you are waiting for your campaigns to kick into gear. This is why in the beginning, you likely won't need to spend much more than 10 to 15 minutes a week checking to see how your ads are actually doing.

Now, I know that we live in a refresh your browser, immediate gratification kind of world. So, it's worth keeping this point in mind: Amazon ads take time. Refreshing your browser every hour is a waste of valuable keyword research or writing time. So, when it's time to check your ads for the week, you can use an online timer like eggtimer.com to keep yourself from fixating too long. We'll go into what you actually do during these data analysis sessions a bit later in the book. Total time commitment for Weeks One through Four: 10 to 15 minutes. Total time commitment for Weeks Four and beyond: 20 to 30 minutes.

Knowing what actions to take may not be very helpful if you have no idea where this weekly time is going to come from. So, how do you make time for these tasks? There are two major options here. You either have to stop something you regularly do, or you have to improve your skill and efficiency with that task.

There are so many different aspects of book marketing that you can focus on in a given moment. At Best Page Forward and Author Ad School, we're always looking for what items we can get rid of to make time for what's really important. For every potentially profitable action, there is a time suck waiting to stop you from making progress. If an action is not contributing to either the enjoyment of your writing or the profitability of your marketing, then it's probably worth getting rid of.

A little note on writing time. It is our hope that unless you've been writing seven hours a day (I know, we can all dream, right?) that you don't have to sacrifice much writing time to fit in ad creation. But the reality of the situation is that you may not have very much time to spare in a given week.

One of the fastest ways to create time is to dial back on using social media. It's hard to do when it gives so many of us the satisfaction of instant gratification and makes us feel connected to others when being an author can be so solitary. But realistically, you don't need to check your Facebook feed every time you're bored and pick up your cell phone. Cutting out some of those habitual check-ins is the easiest way to free up time for marketing.

Six-figure cozy mystery author Trixie Silvertale has one of my favorite stories related to making time for her book marketing. She was actually the project manager of Best Page Forward when she saw that her Amazon ads were starting to work for a brand new "written-to-market" series. With her royalties-tide turning, she knew she had to invest more into the book marketing.

Trixie chose to leave "one of her favorite jobs ever" with my team to focus on writing and ads. She's now consistently above $10,000 in royalties per month. Sometimes, you have to cut things out of your schedule to focus entirely on what's making you the most publishing profit.

In general, we recommend ditching both unprofitable and time-sucking activities followed by making your writing and marketing schedule as efficient as humanly possible. But if you have exhausted all of those angles and there's still not enough time to research keywords and make new ads, then you may have to trade some of your writing time in the early days. It's not ideal to sacrifice some of your creative moments, but sometimes you've got to do what you've got to do to forge your path forward in this self-publishing world.

* * *

Chapter 2 Exercises

1. Open the notes document that you created in Chapter One and write down the answers to the following questions.

2. Brainstorm when you might be able to set aside one to two hours a week to work on your ads. What days and times will you be free on a regular basis?.

3. Think about one difficulty you might have to deal with to set this time aside. How would you get around it?

* * *

It had been a week since Erin and I had chatted. And to her credit, she had created 10 new ads for her books.

"You're doing good work here. I'm sure it was hard to squeeze in," I said.

"Everything is hard," she said. "But I figured I didn't want to waste your time and mine. It wasn't so bad once I got the hang of it."

I nodded. "Everything takes a little bit of practice. Let me take a quick peek at your numbers here." I glanced at the top row of her Amazon ads campaign spreadsheet. It showed me all her stats like number of clicks, ad spend, and more. I noticed that in just a few days, she'd already received 13 clicks on her ads. There was only one problem.

"Erin, it says you've spent around $14 so far on these ads. I think that means you bid way more than $0.39 here. Do you know what happened?"

"Oh, that makes total sense," she said. "I thought your numbers were just recommendations, so I used what I thought would work instead. After all, if I spend more money, I'll get results faster, right?"

It was a mistake I had seen other students make before. Thankfully, it wasn't too late for her to turn it around. "How important is profit to you Erin?"

Her breath caught a bit as she spoke. "It's very, *very* important."

"Then I want you to listen very closely to what I'm going to tell you," I said. "Raising your bids through the roof won't earn you a profit. Unfortunately, all it'll do is pour your money down the drain."

CHAPTER 3

HOW DO I SET UP AMAZON ADS FOR MAXIMUM PROFIT?

Like many authors I've worked with, Erin didn't have one type of book to promote. She'd started out with her passion, a science fiction trilogy. When that hadn't sold nearly as well as she'd hoped, she'd moved into nonfiction and life coaching for a bit. Her current effort was a small-town romance series with covers that seemed to be in pretty decent shape.

"Those three romances don't really feel like my books," she'd said on more than one occasion. "I didn't have pictures of Fabio on my wall growing up. I had Han Solo."

I flipped through her ads from highest spend to lowest.

"So, what gave you the romance bug?" I asked.

"I got really tired of selling five copies a month," she said. "But I guess the joke is on me. Unless I bid $1 on these ads, I still sell about the same amount."

There it was again. I'd seen this thought process play out for thousands of authors when they didn't get the results they wanted right away. But that need for speed presented a huge monetary problem.

"Look Erin, I'm not going to lie to you either—"

"It looks like the shoe is on the other foot," she said.

"Will telling Amazon they can take more of your money get you clicks and impressions faster?" I asked. "It absolutely will. But if the math doesn't check out, you'll always spend more on ads than you'll make in royalties. That means you'll never make a profit. This is why low bids are so important."

Erin sighed. "I've tried that strategy before. I think I heard actual crickets chirping from my computer."

There was always a bit of interpretation at this stage of the coaching game. Had she tried for a day? A week? With one ad? With a dozen?

"You know the old saying," I said. "If at first you don't succeed—"

"Open a fortune cookie? I know I didn't have a coach watching my every move the last time I tried ads, but I can't wait around all month for these stupid things to wake up," she said. "There's just too much resting on this."

I could tell she had the weight of the world on her shoulders. Most authors did.

"Waiting is a frustrating but necessary part of running ads," I said. "You have no choice but to bid low enough that you can actually make at least a little bit of profit."

"And how long will that take, Mr. Guru?"

"It takes as long as it takes. Hopefully, a few months," I said. "Maybe more."

She shook her head. "I really, truly need something faster."

My pulse started to race. Patience and prudence weren't the flashy selling points of the "hot new thing," but Amazon ads were never about being cool. They were slow, steady, and replicable. But I knew from experience that if I didn't convince her to keep trying, I would probably lose her.

"I know you want results today. Heck, I know that you wish you had 'em last month or the month before. I get that," I said. "But I've seen a lot of authors get great results from these ads. And absolutely none of them had success when they rushed. Trying to go too fast actually hurt their chances of success."

"You don't understand," she said. "I need this to start working today."

I nodded. "It can. I've seen it work. And if we can get these numbers right from the start," I said, "we can try to make every single click earn you some profit."

* * *

I've always been a fan of the 'triangle of value' metaphor. People often want something fast, cheap, and high quality. But usually, you're only able to get one or two of those things at a time. If you try to do Amazon ads fast, you probably aren't going to be able to get them cheap (and you may end up sacrificing some of the quality as well).

There are many strategies with these Amazon ads that involve bidding higher to get the attention of the almighty algorithm. I get where they're coming from, but I don't like the idea of you or any other author losing money with every single reader who makes it to your book's sales page.

Let's say you're trying to sell a $4.99 e-book. When a wonderful reader decides to purchase your title, you'll receive 70% of the royalties (or approximately $3.75). In this example, let's also assume that it takes about 10 clicks on your Amazon ads for someone to buy the book.

This means you get $3.75 for every 10 clicks, so if you pay more than $3.75, you won't have profit in your pocket.

Diving even deeper with a bit of a calculation, if you divide $3.75 royalties per sale by 10 clicks, that's the maximum you can spend to earn a profit.

$3.75/10 = 37.5 cents per click for your maximum bid (i.e. $0.37 or lower required for profit).

But if you were to run your ads at $0.40 or $0.50 bids...

You'd keep losing money on average throughout the life of your ad.

This is why lower bids are extremely important to help you maintain profit with your marketing.

Note: As you may have noticed on the other side of this equation, it's also essential to have as few clicks as possible for readers to buy your book. This is something we call *conversion rate*, and we'll get into how to improve this stat later in the book.

For our purposes in this book, we recommend using certain bids or lower to improve your chances of profitability. For series starters and box sets, we go with 39 cents, and for standalones we recommend 34 cents. If you write children's books or low content titles like journals, then you can start at 15 cents.

So, what are some of the pros of running ads with low bids?

1. Faster is Not Always Better

When it comes to your ads, there is nothing wrong with dipping your toes in the shallow end of the pool.

When you bid higher on any advertising platform (Facebook, Amazon, BookBub, etc.), you can get them to spend more of your money more quickly. It's also very easy for that cash to leave your account so fast, you have no idea what that money even accomplished.

I know profitable author advertisers who have had some of the same ad campaigns running for three or more years. That's over 1,000 consecutive days of consistently profitable clicks (and readers) coming to their books.

If you want something to last that long, then you don't want to rush it.

Looking at Amazon ads not like a quick win, but more like a long-term investment, will give you a better chance at success.

2. Ads Still Get Seen with Lower Bids

There's a misconception going around about ads that they're only shown if they have high bids. But the price for bids is only one of two factors for how ads get placed by Amazon's software, which is commonly known as *the algorithm.*

The other consideration is how relevant your book is to the other titles you're advertising on.

Essentially, if your book isn't a magical wizard school novel, then you shouldn't be advertising to Harry Potter books. You only want to advertise to books that are in your genre or tell a similar story. That means if your book is in an extremely small niche, you likely won't want to cast your net very wide.

For example, I have a series of writing workbooks for kids. I pretty much only run ads to other workbooks for children around the same age and grade as my books. Despite having bids of $0.39 or lower, I still receive hundreds of profitable clicks per month.

Relevancy is so important that we'll have an entire chapter devoted to it later, but make sure to remember this point: **having a high bid isn't the only way to get your ads seen**. If there's a method that gets you more affordable attention on your books (even if it's a little slower), then it makes total sense for you to spend less money to get the same results.

3. If You Pay Too Much, You'll Never Profit

I want to talk about this point on a larger scale.

There are scary companies out there that charge authors over $10,000 for a so-called "publishing package" to get a book cover, copyediting, and publication. The authors who use these services start their book publishing journey in the hole by about ten grand. Since many books don't come close to earning that much, they'll always be playing catch up and never make back their huge investment.

The same can be true for authors who spend top dollar on a cover, developmental editing, and other expenses. They think that by spending more money, they'll automatically make it back instantly. Unfortunately, that's rarely the case.

It's true that the most successful authors in self-publishing spend a lot of money to market and promote their books. But that comes well after they've already found success by pulling themselves up by their bootstraps (a.k.a. avoiding large expenses).

In one case, an author we worked with was already having great success with her nonfiction books with over $8,000 a month in royalties. But her profit numbers with ads weren't so strong. She tried a few different methods until she stumbled on the low-bid, high-profit system we teach in our free ad challenges.

Despite sticking with low bids, she and her husband bought into Amazon ads without bidding higher than 40 cents. Through hundreds of campaigns set up over months of work, she was able to grow beyond $8,000 to over $18,000 a month consistently in royalties. Sometimes, you can see major results without bidding through the roof. After all, why pay more for clicks if you don't have to?

To give yourself the best chance of long-term publishing achievement, you'll want to spend less money whenever you can. This means keeping your ads profitable through *optimized conversion rate* (coming in a later chapter) and through lower bids on your ads.

Let's tackle another homework assignment before we get back to our story.

* * *

Chapter 3 Exercises

1. How much do you earn when you sell a copy of the main book you're advertising? Get out a calculator or check your book details to find the answer. Write down the answer to this and all the questions in your notes document.

2. If you've run ads on Amazon previously, what were some of the bids you used when telling the site how much you would pay for your clicks?

3. If you sold 1 book for every 10 clicks (the number you earn in #1 divided by 10) would that amount be higher or lower than what you bid in #2?

4. Based on your answer, do you think your ads have a high or low chance of being profitable in the long run?

* * *

It had been a couple of weeks since my last meeting with Erin. Since I hadn't heard from her in the interim, I held onto hope that she'd have a positive result to latch onto.

Amazon ads weren't an overnight success kind of platform, but plenty of authors grew pretty frustrated if they didn't see some excitement within a few days.

"Read 'em and weep," she said upon showing me her ad dashboard. "I think it's about time for me to fold."

After scrolling through her campaigns, I saw additional impressions and clicks, but very little movement in the sales column. Now, I needed to see the rest of the story.

"I'm really glad you're getting more clicks," I said. "And you're paying less for them, so I chalk that up to a win, actually."

Erin couldn't help but send a little side eye my way. "You're telling me that I'm still throwing money down a hole, but I'm being smarter about it? I wouldn't call that a victory."

"I need you to go to one more website for me," I said.

I pasted a link in the chat, and she brought up the info.

My internal anticipation grew as the final pixel loaded. And when I saw exactly what I was hoping for, I couldn't help but smile.

"Okay," she said. "What do you seem so tickled about?"

"Oh, I just noticed something."

"What do you see?" she asked.

"Nothing to stress about," I said. "Just a telltale sign that your ads are working better than you think."

CHAPTER 4
HOW DO I KNOW IF MY ADS ARE WORKING?

During coaching calls, I often asked my students if I could take over their screen so that I could click and scroll to the right information with ease. Unfortunately, Erin had her own thoughts about what pages I should be looking at.

"Assuming you still want my candor here, I have no idea why I need to check a second site when it seems like a pretty obvious failure," she said. "There's a big fat $0 in the sales column. How could that mean anything else than a new reason to bang my head against the nearest wall?"

I repositioned the windows on Erin's computer to show the ad dashboard on the left side of the screen and the other site on the right side.

"This is one of the most important concepts of advertising," I said. "We already said that you need consistent profit to keep the ads successful. But you also need to know where to look to find those numbers."

I zoomed in on the KDP Reports Dashboard, an Amazon site that showed an estimate of how much you've earned from your books over a given time period. The webpage was one of the best ways to quickly tell if royalties have dropped or risen on a particular day, week, or month.

I continued. "The ad dashboard on its own doesn't give you all the information you need to know if your ads are working."

Erin wrinkled her forehead. "That makes absolutely no sense," she said. "There's a column that says sales. There's no money in it. Doesn't that mean that ads have burned a hole in my digital pocket?"

I readjusted the page to make sure the key stats had been highlighted.

"It could mean that, but there's a major issue," I said. "The dashboard sometimes misses sales that could have come directly or indirectly from the ads. Some authors I've worked with see a major increase in royalties after starting ads without seeing much of a change in this sales column. That's why I tend to call this column *tracked sales*."

Erin studied the two pages. "So, you're telling me this number that most of the author world uses to figure out if their ads work... is broken?"

I made sure to choose my words carefully. I'd seen plenty of authors multiply their royalties when this concept sunk in. Whether it was today or far off down the line, I wanted to make sure Erin saw this clearly.

"We're not sure if it's broken or if ads just have more indirect benefits than we ever guessed," I said. "But when I've seen authors ignore the sales column on the ad dashboard and focus entirely on overall profit, they often see that number grow from month to month," I said. "And I think the majority of us authors would be happy to have more profit."

For a brief moment, Erin shed the teensiest bit of her prickly demeanor. I think she wanted to believe me at that moment because she could see the potentially positive future if I was right.

"I'm a little shell-shocked here, Guru. There's nothing quite like having the world turned upside down. Let's say I go down this Yellow Brick Road you're describing here," she said. "What did you see in my royalties that made you think the ads were working?"

I smiled and dragged the mouse cursor across the screen in a straight line.

"This line represents $20 a day in total royalties," I said. "According to this, you had one day over $20 before you started the ads." I continued the cursor's path. "But after you set up the ads, even with that $0 listed in the tracked sales column, you had three days at $20 or higher."

Erin blinked. "I hadn't noticed that," she said. "So, it's either a fluke... or the ads are actually doing something."

Internally, I couldn't help but play a few bars of the song "Celebration."

"You're right," I said. "And if there's even a remote chance that the ads are responsible, we need to take it a little bit on faith to see if the profitable trend continues."

* * *

When I first started running Amazon ads in 2016, I looked at the stat columns on the ad dashboard and assumed all my campaigns were doing terribly. After all, my orders were next to nothing, and my sales and advertising cost of sale (ACoS) were worse than some of the teachers told me it should be.

My moment of truth came when I ran two ad campaigns to a multi-author anthology called *Once Upon a Happy Ending*.

According to the ad dashboard, I spent $9 in ad spend for every $1 in sales I earned, giving me a 900% ACoS and not a lot of hope. But when I brought up a sales tracker like today's KDP Reports, my royalties for that book were three times higher than my ad spend.

I was making $3 for every $1 I put into the ad. Over about a two-year period, I was able to spend $7,000 to make over $21,000 in royalties. But the ad dashboard made it look like the two ads were crashing and burning.

Since that day, I've shared this concept with tens of thousands of authors. And those that kept up with the ads for several months tended to see the same phenomenon I had.

This is why I developed the *split screen method*. Here's how it works. You bring up the ad dashboard on one side of your screen and you open the KDP Reports Dashboard (or your favorite sales reporting software) on the other side of your screen. You set the dates for each to make sure you're comparing apples to apples, and then you compare the two most important numbers: ad spend and royalties.

If your royalties are higher than your ad spend, then you have a profit. If your ad spend is higher than your royalties, then you have a loss. I usually start by looking at the overall picture (total ad spend and total royalties). From there, I can check on individual books or entire series to see if those are profitable.

Now, it's worth mentioning that some authors really push back on this concept. I often hear two main arguments.

Argument One

The first criticism is that this system ignores the concept of organic sales. Organic sales are when readers just stumble upon your book through search or randomness and purchase your title.

They say, "You don't want to overestimate how well your ads are doing because then you won't have as good a return."

These authors absolutely have a point. Amazon will likely never share the data of how we get so-called organic sales and where they come from.

So, there are two main options here:

1. Assume the ad dashboard is right and that all sales that don't show up on the sales column are organic.
2. Assume that the ad dashboard isn't showing the whole picture and that all royalties on the KDP Reports Dashboard come from your ads.

Here's the main reason I've chosen Option 2. More authors than I can count have come to me and said, "Bryan, I believed in Option 1 and turned off my ads because the sales column had nothing. That's when my royalties dropped like a stone."

This pattern for authors turning off their so-called "poor performers" showed me that it was better to overestimate ad performance than it was to underestimate (and see your royalties fall away to nothing).

Why does this happen? Amazon Ads track sales and KENP (Kindle Edition Normalized Pages a.k.a. Kindle Unlimited pages read) that occur within 14 days of an ad click. You receive KENP when a Kindle Unlimited borrower begins reading your book (which works out to less than half a cent per page).

If a reader clicks on an ad and doesn't buy but they purchase three weeks later when the book shows up on their recommendations, then the sale won't show up in your Sales or KENP column. If a reader clicks on an ad and downloads the sample to read later and eventually goes on to buy the book more than two weeks later, then the ad won't track the sale either. If you run an ad to your book in KDP Select (a.k.a. exclusive to Amazon) but they don't start flipping the pages until three weeks later, then those pages read won't show up on your ad dashboard.

In these cases and a variety of other scenarios, you'll still get the royalties, but the ad will look like it's performing worse than it actually is. I choose to assume that the ad dashboard isn't showing the whole picture because it helps me to account for any sales or Kindle Unlimited borrows that fall through the cracks.

Argument Two

The other argument these authors make is that you have to believe the ad dashboard because otherwise, you don't know which ads to keep running and which ads to turn off.

Personally, I rarely turn off ads for a book that's earning higher royalties than I'm spending on ads. But when you're trying to figure out the health of your ads, here are three things that I look for:

1. Royalties Going Up

This should be no surprise based on what I mentioned above. Much like in the example with Erin, you want to see if there are any obvious peaks that weren't there prior to the ads. You'll also want to see if there are fewer low royalty days than normal (i.e. see if the floor of your royalties has risen). You want to look for any daily evidence that the ads are having some kind of impact.

Of course, once you have a month or more of data, you'll want to look at the overall profitability using the split screen method. But at first, when you're new to the platform and your fear is at its highest, seeing those daily hints of potential success may be just enough to keep you going.

2. Throwing Tracked Sales & Tracked KENP a Bone

While I often harp on the importance of ignoring the sales column on the ad dashboard (a.k.a. tracked sales), it's even more telling when you have the best of both worlds. If you're getting tracked sales and tracked KENP from your ads **and** you're seeing royalties go up, you can be confident your campaigns are performing well.

Even though this is the most obvious indicator that ads are working well for you, there's a reason I don't have it first in this section. Plenty of authors who don't see these tracked sales see some movement on the royalties side. The lesson here is don't be too worried if you don't see sales and KENP piling up on the ad dashboard.

One of the stats that authors tend to follow for ad success today is ACoS or Advertising Cost of Sale. This is a figure that represents your Ad Spend divided by your Tracked Sales on your ad dashboard. Many of these authors ignore the royalties over on the KDP Reports page and focus entirely on ACoS being 50% or lower, which would represent spending 50 cents to earn $1 in gross sales (before Amazon takes their cut).

But ACoS isn't nearly as important as profit. If this stat is higher than 50% but you see that overall you're earning more in royalties than you're spending on ads, then I find it's worth keeping the ads running.

No matter what stats you see, the most important one remains profit. You can't pay your car loan with a low ACoS, but you can pay it down with higher monthly profit.

3. Sales Rank Going Up

When you have a book in Kindle Unlimited (Kindle Select), there are two key moments when a reader borrows your book. Within hours of a reader putting your title in their KU pile, you'll see an improvement of your book's *sales rank* (the number decreases when your rank improves, like 250,000 to 100,000). But you don't actually see any royalties until that person begins reading the book.

This is why if you have KU titles you need to pay attention to your sales rank, especially in the early days of running your ads. You can keep track of your rank using the Amazon Author Central platform.

In my free Author Ad Challenges, we touch on this important concept only briefly, to keep things as simple as we can for beginners. Essentially, if you don't see an improvement in royalties right away and you aren't getting any tracked sales or tracked KENP, then you'll want to see if sales rank improved for the books you're advertising.

For example, if your book was in the 400,000 range before ads and improved to the 70,000 range, this may be a result of the ads.

It's tough to continue running ads when no money has come in, but it's important to remember that improvement in sales rank now will likely mean readers will start reading and getting you some sweet, sweet page reads and income over the next couple of weeks.

It's partly because of this delayed payout from Kindle Unlimited borrows that it's very important to run ads for at least 3-4 weeks and/or 100 clicks before you make any major changes in your campaigns.

When you see any of the three above indicators that your ads might be working, you should take it as a sign that the Amazon ads platform might just be worth it for you. There are plenty of factors to consider later on about whether you can sustain the profit. But if you quit while you're ahead, you may never find out if the platform could have been a game changer for you.

When I began experimenting with ads in 2016, I threw everything but the kitchen sink at them to make them work. No matter what I did, my ad dashboard stats seemed to paint a very bleak picture. At one point, my ads even said I was spending over $7 to earn a single dollar in sales. But when I looked over at my actual royalties on the KDP Reports dashboard, I saw a very different story. In reality, my ad spend was only a third of the money that was coming in, which meant I could spend $1 and make $3 with ease.

Of course, I had to test this on a greater scale with the book I mentioned earlier. I poured over $7,000 in over the next 12 months to see if the trend would continue. According to the ad dashboard, my campaigns got even worse with $9 spend for each $1 in sales. But at the end of it all, I'd earned $21,000+ in royalties for the $7,000 ad spend. That was a $14,000 profit that would've been lost had I failed to look at my bottom line.

Sometimes, you need to take a view of the whole picture of your KDP royalties to see if your ads are actually working.

* * *

Chapter 4 Exercises

1. Open the KDP Reports Dashboard and the Author Central page and start poking around to learn more about your books' royalties and sales ranks for the past few months.

2. Based on what you've done to market your books (whether Amazon ads or not), do you see any pattern between your marketing efforts and an improvement in royalties or rank?

3. Write down some steps you might take to stay patient when determining if your ads are working.

* * *

A couple of weeks went by, and I read Erin's colorful reports along the way. While her tone remained consistent throughout, it appeared as though her stats were headed in the right direction. Her romance numbers seemed the most promising with over two-dozen clicks and even some tracked KENP (pages read).

As our next meeting began, I even detected a sliver of sunshine poking through.

"I'm really liking what I see with some of these ads," I said. "You're not always going to see every book succeed right away but having one series improve this early on is great!"

I detected a bit of hesitancy from my coaching student.

"That sounds like pretty good news," she said. "I'll take progress over nothing. And just to make sure the other books start moving too, I did up a few of my bids here and there."

As often as authors said that profit was their #1 goal, it was surprising how frequently they took actions that completely went against taking home more money.

"Let's check the damage then," I said. "But I do have to mention once again that you may pay too much for those clicks."

Scrolling through, I saw bids ranging from $0.50 to $1.05 for both her sci-fi series starters and her nonfiction standalone titles. I verbally ran through the math of the $1.05 bid scenario until she cut me off.

"Look, it's simple," she said. "If higher bids mean I'm going to get more eyeballs, then I have to increase my bids. It's the only way."

I took a breath. "It's actually 50% of the way."

She narrowed her eyes. "What do you mean 50% of the way?"

I tabbed over to an Amazon book sales page and a carousel of sponsored ads.

"Amazon doesn't just place ads with the bid price," I said. "There's a whole other criteria they use. It's actually kind of our secret weapon to lower costs."

"Trust me, I have my listening ears on for this," she said.

I detected a hint of relief in her voice and hoped that perhaps this next lesson would finally get through to her.

CHAPTER 5

HOW DO I GET MY ADS SEEN WITH LOW BIDS?

Authors like Erin have always impressed me. Despite the work of running the household, shuttling kids around, and somehow holding onto her sanity, she had also written hundreds of thousands of words. With each step she took toward potential future profitability, I had more and more hope that the effort would be worth the time and energy she'd put in.

Later on during the call, I dove deeper into some of Erin's ad campaigns to check for areas of improvement. I opened the targeting page of a particularly stuffed Sponsored Product Category ad.

"Can you explain your thoughts on using this number of categories?" I asked.

"You're very kind to assume there was logic involved. I heard that each category you pick lets you target the entire genre," she said. "So, I figured combining them would give the ad the best chance of getting seen."

The ad, which targeted her struggling sci-fi series, included categories related to her subgenre. But I also spied fantasy coming of age, female detectives, and even American fiction in the mix.

"Oh, you'll definitely get the ad seen in the short-term," I said. "But you may run into more than a few problems in the long-run."

Erin grabbed a sticky note off her desk and crumbled it into a tight ball. "Oh, happy days!"

"It's okay to be frustrated," I said. "I get that way about this kind of stuff sometimes, too."

She shook her head. "These ads are driving me up the wall. It's like every instinct I have here is the opposite of correct. Doesn't it make sense to try to get my book out to as many readers as possible?"

I leaned toward my laptop. "Amazon is all about its customers, and some of its customers read books," I said. "But not all of them read in every genre. Some of them only want to read cozy mysteries and others only want to read epic fantasy. And if you target the wrong readers, it makes Amazon's algorithms unsure about what kind of book you've actually written."

Erin squeezed the crumbled note tighter. "So, I need to make the algorithms happy."

"Yes," I said.

"Then I can pay less money for each click?" she asked.

"Yes," I replied.

She looked up to the ceiling before her eyes returned to me. "Alright then. I suppose I talk to a hockey puck every day to get the weather and a phone to sort out directions. What's one more computer?" she asked. "How on Earth do I make the algorithms happy?"

"By following one of the most essential concepts of advertising," I said. "You need to understand the importance of *relevancy*."

* * *

We've seen over 30,000 authors through our free challenges. That's given me and my team a broad perspective on the kinds of authors

.ng to run Amazon ads. Erin was hardly the only person I'd seen attempting to combine different ideas from a variety of ad philosophies. And the expertise and intelligence of those teachers was clear in their instruction. However, our own data seemed to diverge from their methods in a few key areas.

It's easy to get Amazon to spend your money if you bid high enough, but since we're looking for profit, we wanted to find another way. In the early days of the challenges, we weren't entirely sure why some ads would get clicks at lower bids while others barely moved the needle.

That's when former Amazon ads employee and stellar educator Janet Margot shared the key component to the author community. She helped to introduce the other part of the equation: the need for your ad targets to be relevant.

Relevancy is another word for similarity. When we choose targets for our Amazon ad campaigns in the form of keywords and categories, we want to make sure these terms closely relate to our book. For certain niche topics in the nonfiction realm, this can be a challenge. Fortunately, for most genre fiction, there are still plenty of books that are similar enough to yours for effective ad targeting.

Why do we want to pay careful attention to the relevancy of our keywords and categories? It's because using high bids is not the only way to get your ad seen. Amazon's algorithm also factors your ad's relevancy into how often it gets impressions and clicks. Even ads using high-roller bids like $1 or higher will start getting fewer and fewer readers to your page if they're targeting terms that don't connect with your book.

The hope is to find a sweet spot with a bid that's just high enough to be seen, but not so high that it prevents you from earning a profit.

How do you determine whether or not a keyword or category is relevant? Let's take a look at the five rules of relevant research for your Amazon ads.

1. Know Thy Genre

One of the first rules of writing in a particular genre is to study what that category actually looks like on Amazon. Too many beginner authors write a book and then start looking around to see what Frankenstein's monster of stylistic choices they've created. As you write more books and dive deeper into the business side of self-publishing, you'll learn to do that research in the beginning.

Readers have certain expectations of a genre book (i.e. Romance will have a happy ending, cozy mystery will have an amateur female sleuth, etc.). It's extremely helpful to know these expectations when you're writing the book, but it also makes a big difference when you're advertising. If your book fits what readers want when they're looking for a certain type of book, then it makes sense to advertise to that target.

You can and should consider running ads to the 5-10 categories or fewer that would fit your book like a glove. You can also find the book titles of novels or nonfiction that are similar enough to your work that they'd make sense to be purchased by the same kind of reader (i.e. showing up in your also-boughts). You can also target the words and phrases readers would search if they're trying to find a book just like yours.

To know which categories fit, which titles connect, and which search terms make sense, it helps significantly if you know your genre inside and out.

That means studying the Top 100 Bestsellers lists of your categories, searching for your own book by keyword, and reading books related to yours to keep up with the genre you hope to succeed in.

When you truly understand what readers want to get out of your book, it's a lot easier to find relevant targets.

2. Ads Need Editing Before They're Launched

Gathering keywords for your ad campaigns is like writing the first draft of your book. You're not going to keep every word you've found for the "final draft" that you send out into the world. Sometimes, you've got to make some cuts based on our favorite buzz word of the chapter... *relevancy*.

This isn't a huge issue when you're brainstorming different keywords to put into your ad. But later in the book, where we'll discuss gathering keywords in bulk using certain types of software, it's essential to make some cuts before you launch the ad. Otherwise, terms that are too dissimilar to your book will crop up. If enough of those make it into your campaign, then Amazon's algorithm may not show your low bid ad as much as a campaign it deems more relevant.

This is why you must edit your ads prior to publication.

3. Don't Target Everything

It's very tempting to create ads that could be shown to almost every reader who might even think about reading in your genre. "There's a character who's 17 in my book, so I'm going to target coming of age" or "My protagonist is Australian, so I'm going to choose Oceanic fiction" etc. As a result, we see authors add 10, 15, 20, or even 30+ categories to the same Sponsored Product Category ad.

But while we think we're making a simple choice by giving more readers the opportunity to see our ads, we're actually reducing the ad's chance of effectiveness. One of our responsibilities as advertisers on Amazon is to train the almighty algorithm to know what we've written. We do this upon publication with our own keywords, categories, title, subtitle, and blurb, but we also do it through our discount promos and our Amazon ads (what kind of books we target).

Training the algorithm the right way gives us a better chance of long-term success. But just like the confused mind of a reader says "No" to buying your book, a confused algorithm will have no idea how to promote your title.

Choosing fewer but more related categories for your ads will improve your odds of advertising (and publishing) success.

4. It's Not a Popularity Contest

We get so excited when there's a book related to ours that's extremely popular. Maybe you wrote in dystopian young adult to take advantage of *The Hunger Games* or middle grade fantasy to tap into that magical

Harry Potter audience. But if something becomes a megahit, the chances are that everyone and their mother have purchased the title because it was popular (not necessarily because they read that genre all the time).

And while you may temporarily get more traffic if you target the buzz book of the month, the readers who make up that audience will likely be too broad to be effective.

For example, my young adult superhero novel was proving relatively profitable (especially when you factored in readers making it to book 2, 3, and beyond) until a few keywords went haywire. I noticed my number of impressions and clicks triple overnight without an improvement in royalties or sales rank. When I looked into the offending ad, I discovered that the culprit was the keyword "Spiderman" that had blown up in conjunction with the first Tom Holland *Spider-Man* movie.

Now, you might be thinking, "That's good news! With a superhero movie out, maybe readers are looking for a teenage superhero to read about."

The logic is sound, until you remember that Amazon is a platform for all buyers and not just readers. Shoppers looking for Spider-Man toys, socks, and lunch boxes were causing my ad to get tons of views from people who weren't hungry readers. Without much to show for the ad spend, I opted to pause that particular keyword.

The search term was simply too popular and not relevant enough to keep running.

5. Take Your Time

From a data nerd perspective, seeing 30,000+ authors try out the Amazon ads platform allows my team and I to see a ton of information. This has allowed us to spot trends, try new things, and improve our teaching. Without fail, there's one mistake that authors make every single challenge we run: accidentally bidding too high.

As we recommend most authors create 5-10 new ads overall per week, it's easy to want to rush through the process. But when you try to go speedy, it's easy to make a mistake. And when you're the one setting how much you're going to pay, your error can cost you part of your marketing budget.

This is why you need to double- and triple-check your ad before you click the Create Campaign button. For auto ads, you have to adjust your bid down from $0.75 in just one place. But with category and keyword ads, you need to change your bid twice (in the default and custom tabs) in order to ensure your bid is set properly.

Also, there are buttons labeled "Apply" and "Apply All" that will quickly add the keyword or category's suggested bid to your target. Unfortunately, the suggested bid is usually much higher than what we'd recommend. One accidental click of the Apply buttons, and your bid will suddenly rise.

This is why we should pair our slow and steady ads with a slow and steady ad creation process. Always carefully review the details before publishing the ad. Zoom into the screen if you need to. Verbally call out all the ways you've ensured the ad is correct. Do whatever is necessary to make sure you've gotten the ad right before you click Publish.

GR Lyons had been running ads for months when he decided to take the process more seriously. After going back through the keywords he'd chosen for his campaigns, he realized that they weren't nearly as relevant as he'd first thought. The same was true with some of the categories his books were in on the Amazon marketplace. He made it his top priority to get his targeting back in order before he got back in the habit of making regular ads.

The results were slow and steady, but within a few months, his royalties began to climb. With his concentration on relevancy, only targeting books similar to his, he began regularly eclipsing four figures a month. Sometimes, getting in touch with the right kind of targets for your books and running regular ads can help you reach and exceed your goals.

It's worth considering that once we've made automatic ads and we've exhausted the number of relevant category ads, we'll be seeking keywords each week to make new ads. Ideally, you'll be able to find over 500 keywords per week to spread out across five ads (with about 100 keywords per ad). How do we collect those terms using a system that takes less time? That's exactly what we'll go into in the following chapter.

* * *

Chapter 5 Exercises

1. Visit the Amazon website and start searching for your book using a variety of keywords.

2. Write down in your notes document which keywords actually lead you to your book and which ones don't.

3. What are some of the other books you find while you're attempting to locate your own? Would you call them relevant to your title? Write down your findings.

4. Take a look at the ads that pop up as *Sponsored* when you're searching. Do you see any trends popping up with certain keywords? Write down your thoughts.

* * *

Our next two sessions seemed to crawl by as Erin had very little to say. I followed along on her screen and saw her using more relevant categories and keywords, but she seemed to be going through the motions with little enthusiasm.

"So, how does the research and ad creation part make you feel?" I asked.

Her reaction was delayed. "What? Oh. Fine, I guess," she said. "We can keep making ads. Don't worry about me."

I couldn't help but press. "I've heard some authors say they start to enjoy this part after a while. Maybe it'll become a fun escape for you at some point?"

She waved me off. "It's not the ads. I'm just so tired and there's so much going on. It's like there's a ticking clock floating above my head. It seems like there's so much to learn to get things right and I'm out of time."

It was the first time I could see defeat wash across Erin's face.

"I know that I'm just your contest-appointed book marketing coach and I don't know you so well yet, but it definitely seems like there's some major stress happening here," I said. "Is there something going on?"

"My husband lost his job," she said in a hushed voice. "He got three months of severance pay, thank goodness. We have a few months of savings, but after that ... I don't know what happens next. How the heck am I supposed to write my books, create ads, support my family, and sleep all in the same 24-hour period?"

I took a deep breath. We all have moments where it seems like everything is about to crash down. And it turned out my student was right in the middle of that crisis.

"I'm really sorry, Erin. It stinks having to figure this stuff out while you guys are going through something this major," I said. "If it helps at all, I know that plenty of authors feel that ticking clock above their head."

"I wish it did help," she said. "But maybe now you understand why I keep asking you to switch me to the fast track."

I nodded. "I've worked with a lot of writers who say they need those results yesterday, so I promise I understand. But as far as fitting it all into 24 hours, there are absolutely some tweaks to make it work with your life."

I silently wished there was a faster way for all of this to profitably work, but I took a tiny bit of comfort. I'd seen authors in bad situations before. And I knew that with the right drive and solid weekly work, good things for her books and her life were likely to happen. The slow and steady race was on, while the clock kept ticking.

CHAPTER 6
HOW DO I FIT AD CREATION INTO MY WRITING SCHEDULE?

Five minutes had passed since my meeting with Erin was supposed to begin. As I waited and hoped that the previous talk's revelation wouldn't keep her away, I thought about times in my life when I'd lost my job. The times when the number in my bank account had dwindled. The times where the panic started to take over.

I knew there wasn't much I could do to soothe someone's overwhelming emotions from this sort of thing. But if I could find little breadcrumbs of hope and profit for her along the way, maybe it would be enough for everything to be OK. Maybe we could do it before time ran out.

"Sorry I'm late," she said. "If memory serves me right, I think you were going to tell me how to do this fast?"

I laughed out a bit of the stress.

"Good try," I said. "Remember, speed isn't really an option here. But we can start to make regular, steady progress. And the best way to do that is to research and create ads every week."

"You're killing me, Guru. How much more sleep am I going to need to sacrifice here?"

I shook my head. "No more cutting sleep. What we really need to do is consistently find time for two work sessions. One for ad research and one for ad creation. If you can keep them on your calendar and never skip them, you will continue to make forward progress."

Erin shared her screen to show a calendar that was packed wall-to-wall with work.

"Anything on here that's not shuttling a kid from one place to another is dedicated to my books," she said. "You're telling me I have to bump some of it to work on something that might not even hit for weeks or months? If it does at all."

As a parent myself, I was very sympathetic to her struggle to balance everything.

"You know, marketing your book is kind of like parenting your kids. Writing the book is like getting your babies ready to walk, talk, and go to school. But just because they can do some things on their own now doesn't mean your job is done. You still have to drive them around and set them up for success, and it's the exact same thing with your book. You painstakingly wrote it and now it needs help to get into the hands of your readers. Your kids have a better chance to be solid citizens when you give them the support they need and your book has a better chance to sell when you consistently market it."

She snorted. "Maybe it's the sleep deprivation talking, but that actually made sense. Alright, you've inspired me. Tell me what I need to do."

* * *

As authors, we're beset on all sides by countless tasks we need to accomplish on the writing, editing, formatting, and marketing sides. Completing the word count always seems to get the highest priority, and if that is all the schedule has room for, the marketing simply doesn't get done. Trying to balance everything is a daunting task at times.

Here's the good news: I've seen plenty of authors with full-time jobs, families, or both find the time to consistently make new and profitable ads.

But if we aren't going to sacrifice sleep, then something else needs to go. One of my mentors, Pat Flynn, used to say, "If you say yes to something, then you have to say no to something else." Most authors, and people in general, have activities they're consistently doing that don't have a ton of value.

If we can find the regular work we do that doesn't contribute much to our author profit or success, then we can make room for the ongoing process of Amazon advertising.

But how do we figure out what's worth keeping and what needs to go?

First and foremost, if you rarely see sales or royalties from a certain task that you do on a daily basis, then it's the easiest thing to trim.

For example, social media is a fun way to connect with existing superfans in a launch or Advanced Reader Copy group. However, if you regularly get sucked into scrolling the platform for hours at a time, then you're losing time and energy.

Following the hot new marketing trend may be exciting and give you a sense of "maybe pushing this shiny red button will solve my problems." Unfortunately, the glitter of each popular tactic rarely ends in gold. Chasing these trends is another time-suck that can harm your productivity in the long run.

Lastly, there are countless benefits to continuing education in almost any field. But does it really help when you try to balance taking multiple book marketing courses at the same time? How often do you buy a course and then run out of time to do it?

Sometimes the best thing you can do is push the pause button on learning and focus on action.

In most cases, you're much better off spending the majority of that social media, trend hopping, and secondary learning time on writing and ad creation.

By focusing your attention on fewer things, you'll avoid distractions and make progress more quickly than you would have otherwise.

So, what should our ad research and creation sessions look like?

I tend to divide my Amazon ad work into two separate weekly meetings with myself. In the first, I spend 100% of my time researching new, relevant targets to use in my ads. In the second, I spend 100% of my time actually creating the ads themselves.

I use the divide-and-conquer approach for the same reason I don't write and edit during the same time block: I want to get into a mental flow state so I get faster and more efficient as I go. Think of it like an efficient assembly line that works best when the process is streamlined into its different parts.

Let's dive into three things to keep in mind with a successful research session.

1. Choose a Non-Creative Time

As a rule of thumb, I try to avoid all my "stare at a computer" tasks when I'm writing my first drafts. I'm all about training my brain to be more creative at the same time every day (usually around 5:15 a.m.). I consider this to be sacred scribe time and will never let computer tasks like keyword research take over that slot.

I do this, in part, because fixing my eyes on the screen tends to sap my creative energy. I'm not as likely to get writing done after I take on even the simplest of tasks like posting on social media, answering emails, or researching ads. That's why I'll slot these sessions into the afternoon (usually on a Tuesday or Wednesday for me). This way, I'm able to keep my writing appointments going and I'm able to recover my creative energy by the next morning.

Let's say you only have an hour a day to fit in your writing and all your marketing. You'll want to see what works best for you, but I'd recommend doing the writing for the first 30-45 minutes and save any marketing tasks for the last part of the hour.

It's not important that you get all these ads up immediately. What matters is that you're making small, incremental progress each week toward gaining more control over your book marketing.

2. Make It a Reward

I'm fortunate enough to have a team of wonderful authors who help keep our company running (thank you, BPF writers and Ad Squad!), but this was not always the case. Back when it was just me running the show, there were plenty of mundane tasks of authorhood that kept getting pushed down and off my to-do list.

One of my solutions to the work I didn't find very engaging was to give myself the reward of watching a great show or exciting movie to have on in the background while I worked. And though this isn't a strategy I'd recommend for ad creation (I'll explain why later in this chapter), it's perfectly reasonable to research keywords while you get the opportunity to play.

I pull this off by either getting a show up on my phone or putting it on my work computer and resizing the window to the top right corner of the screen. If you have two monitors, you can probably do this even more effectively than I can. Simply click, copy, paste, and laugh (or cry) while you work.

By syncing up this entertainment with the grunt work of finding more ad targets, you may even start to enjoy the task more. Just remember to set a timer so you don't overrun the time you've set for this task.

3. Use the Tools

Most of the future ads you create will be keyword ads, which means you'll have to go out there and get 100-150 potential targets for each campaign. Since we're shooting for creating five to ten ads per week, that means you'll need 500-1,500 keywords each week. The good news is that there are some very helpful pieces of software out there that may be able to help you cut down significantly on your keyword research time. In fact, in less than an hour you could gather all the keywords you'll need for an entire month of ads.

One tool that many authors have is *Publisher Rocket*, a brainchild of Kindlepreneur's Dave Chesson. We've found this tool is incredibly valuable for researching your 7 KDP Keywords that you use upon publication. It is also very effective for hunting down your book's categories. Having said that, it's not our top choice for ad keyword research because it sometimes adds in too many mainstream popular books.

But if you already have the software and you're willing to spend extra time editing out irrelevant or super-popular keywords, it can be worth testing.

Another tool that's served us well is the *Instant Data Scraper* plug-in, which is free on the Google Chrome browser.

This plug-in allows you to choose any page on the Internet, such as an Amazon search or a Goodreads Listopia list, and "scrape" book titles, author names, and series titles into a spreadsheet. But we do not recommend using everything you scrape without editing it first. That prevents irrelevant keywords from sneaking in since these lists are user-generated.

The tool can be finicky, and it may be stressful at first for folks who wouldn't consider themselves "computer people," but the free price point plus the ability to gather thousands of keywords at a time makes it completely worth the potential headache.

The third and final tool we'll discuss is a new entrant at the writing of this book, and we hope it'll stand the test of time.

The *Also-Boughts Downloader* from Kindletrends is another free plug-in on Google Chrome. This software allows you to download a list of book titles and author names from any Amazon book's sales page. So, if you wanted to grab a list of all the "also-boughts" connected to a bestseller in your genre, this software would allow you to do it.

Using the also-boughts (a.k.a. the titles that readers usually purchased alongside the book that you're browsing) allows you to collect very relevant targets for your ads. And while you always need to trim your list of keywords no matter what, these targets are often the cleanest you can find. After all, also-bought lists are intended to be relevant from the beginning since they've been sorted by Amazon.

Between *Instant Data Scraper's* mass gathering technique and the *Also-Boughts Downloader's* more specific targeting method, you can collect 2,500+ keywords in a single half-hour hunting session without breaking a sweat. With a few focused research sessions per month, you could have more than enough targets for your prescribed five to ten ads per week.

By keeping your creative time sacred, letting yourself have fun, and using these helpful tools, you'll be able to have a very efficient weekly research session.

Now, let's talk about the three steps that go into an ad creation session.

1. Use Your Best Judgement

As you begin what amounts to an editing and publication meeting with yourself, you'll begin to pore over the thousands of keywords you gathered during your research time.

What you'll want to look for here is finding and deleting keywords that are obviously not relevant to your book. Since you can't possibly know every title that fits in your genre, you'll want to remove only the most obvious books that don't belong.

Cut out extremely popular mainstream titles like *Harry Potter* or *The Hunger Games*. Those will get a ton of very expensive clicks that won't convert well and will lose you money.

Next, you'll look for titles that don't sound like they're in your genre (i.e. books that mention space or stars probably won't fit your small-town contemporary romance).

Lastly, you'll see if there's anything that sounds a little off for your genre (i.e. I'll cut comic books out of my superhero novel research because comic readers don't always read novels).

Let me be clear: you *do not* need to go and look up every keyword on Amazon. That will take up way too much time. I encourage you to do your best to remove words that seem like they won't be relevant and don't worry too much if a few slip in here and there.

2. Label Now for Better Research Later

As you set aside your "edited" batches of keywords, you'll want to label your spreadsheet files *and* your ad campaigns appropriately. For example, if you gathered the also-boughts of the book *Ender's Game*, you'd put something like "ABs from EG" as the title of the spreadsheet and your ad.

Why is this important? Well, if you find that an ad is getting nice traction in the form of clicks and tracked sales (more on this later in the book), then it's very helpful to know where you gathered those keywords. By labeling the ads well, you could go back and target the "also-boughts of the also-boughts," giving yourself an opportunity to double down on the success of your campaign.

If you haven't been using ad campaign names in this way, it's not the end of the world. The best time to start a more organized habit is today!

3. Take Your Time and Double-Check Your Work

To compare writing and publishing a novel to ad creation, this stage of the game would be the final proofread. When you set up your ads (approximately 5-10 ads per week toward the book you're focusing on), you need to double- and triple-check that you've set the right amount for your bids.

In our story example, Erin actively went against my recommendation for bidding. But it's also very easy to put in a higher number accidentally.

One reason is that you have to change two types of bids: your *custom bid* and your *default bid*. If you leave one of those two bids at the Amazon-recommended amount of $0.75, then you will pay more than you'd bargained for and it will cut into your profits.

Before you run your campaign, you absolutely have to check that both default and custom bids have been changed for your keyword and category ads (there's only one bid type for the auto ads).

It's nerve-wracking to work on these tasks for the first time because you may wonder if it's always going to be a slog. But just like you used to "hunt and peck" on your keyboard before you were able to type and write faster, you'll start slow and become much more efficient over time.

I met MM romance author Quinn Ward shortly before the 20Books Vegas 2019 conference. I didn't find out until much later that they were on the verge of quitting and had only attended the event out of guilt of not using their ticket. They'd published 20+ books but the royalties just weren't coming in. Amazon ads were the "one more marketing thing" they tried. What followed was one of the greatest demonstrations of dedication I'd seen from an author.

Quinn worked full-time at an ice rink, wrote their books on the side, and volunteered their so-called spare time to help newer members of the author community. Somehow, despite the large number of responsibilities, they found the space to create their 5-10 ads per week to get more impressions and clicks. Occasionally, those hours came late at night with others coming in the carpool lane to pick up their kids.

Within two years of their hard work, they'd gone from under $1,000 a month to becoming a six-figure author. Sometimes when there's no time to do the work, you have to make the time.

Some of the authors we've worked with have actually found that they've enjoyed the process and started to look forward to their weekly ad creation sessions. It can be a very Zen experience when you embrace your inner Zen Lemur.

Creating ads every week is a habit that has helped hundreds of authors earn more profit. In the book *Atomic Habits*, James Clear discusses that identifying as a particular person can help to make the habit stick. So rather than saying, "I have to create ads every week," you can reframe your perspective by stating, "I am an author advertiser." By identifying as an author advertiser, you may be more willing to keep the helpful habit up for the long-term.

* * *

Chapter 6 Exercises

1. Set aside 30-60 minutes twice a week as a recurring event on your calendar.

2. Label one of those sessions as your Keyword Research session and one as your Ad Editing & Creation session.

3. Download the *Instant Data Scraper* and Kindletrends *Also-Boughts Downloader* plug-ins. We've linked to these and other tools in our Links Glossary at BestPageForward.net/Ads.

* * *

Knowing what Erin and her family were going through helped me to better understand the budding author-advertiser in my midst. Over the next couple of weeks, she continued to follow the steps of ad research and creation. She seemed to appreciate the opportunity to binge-watch an old sitcom while she hunted down the terms that would potentially solve her impending financial challenge.

"He's out there looking every single day. Even I'm considering looking, which would mean writing more books might have to go out the window," she said in a defeated tone. "Unless you expect these ads to start kicking into high gear tomorrow."

I took a deep breath. "I wish I knew exactly when things would take off for you. Unfortunately, Amazon's out of stock on actual magic wands. But at least you're taking action to try to make this all work out for you guys."

"Thanks. I just hope all of the advice you're giving me and all this time you're putting in isn't for nothing," she said. "It may not always seem like it, but I actually appreciate what you're doing here."

My heart felt a touch warmer at that. "I don't think it'll be for nothing."

She took a deep breath. "I sure as heck wouldn't mind a sign from above right about now."

As I scanned over her ads on one page and her KDP Reports Dashboard on the other, a little blue line caught my eye.

"Maybe you don't need a sign," I said. "Do you remember how we said you had more $20 royalty days since you started running ads?"

"I seem to remember fewer embarrassing sales days if that's what you mean," she said.

"Here, let me set your KDP Reports for the last 90 days to show you something." I changed the date setting on her dashboard to illustrate my point. "What do you see that's out of the ordinary?"

"Making the old lady work over here. What do I see?" She leaned in closer to the monitor as she squinted at the numbers. "Wait. There's a spike. That's definitely a spike!"

Erin was right. In the last 90 days of selling her books, she'd never eclipsed the $30-a-day mark. Until yesterday.

"It looks like you just had your highest royalty day in the last three months," I said. "What do you think that means?"

A grin crept across her face. "It means the ads are working. The ads are working... and you may not be entirely full of crap!"

"These calls are very motivational for me, Erin," I teased her. "I really should be paying you."

She laughed. "Sorry, not sorry. Does this mean I need to do anything different?"

"Keep doing the work. Keep making more ads. And give yourself a little pat on the back while you're at it," I said. "What are you going to do now?"

"Well, since a trip to Disney World is out of the question, maybe I'll just grab a celebratory latte," she said. "But only after I make my ads for the week, of course."

"Now, that's a stellar answer," I said.

CHAPTER 7

WHY AREN'T SOME ADS WORKING AND WHAT DO I DO ABOUT IT?

I can't help but feel a sense of pride when I see an author doing the work, and Erin had really knuckled down the last couple of weeks. Our calls had more energy than usual, and I might even come close to describing her as perky.

"I finished another five ads this week," she said. "Do I get some kind of prize?"

"The satisfaction of a job well done isn't a prize?" I asked.

She smiled liked she wanted to punch me. I guessed perky wasn't on the menu.

"Look, I'm glad to be taking action. Making ads and checking on stats isn't lighting up my life, but I'm used to it now," she said. "But I'd love to know when we move on from this step."

I raised my eyebrows. "Why do you want to move on?"

"It's tedious. I make ads every week and half of them never do anything. Not a single impression on them," she said. "And if you haven't noticed, my royalties are up but my profit is exactly the same as last month."

Erin had a couple of good points. Around 50% of her ads hadn't even budged, which is normal for low-bid ads, but it's still annoying. And while her royalties were nearing $100 for the month, her actual take-home profit after ad spend was nearly identical to the month before.

"If you had the choice of making $50 randomly or $50 in profit with ads, which would you choose?" I asked.

She pondered for a moment, as if she was trying to figure out the trick.

"I think I see what answer you want me to give," she said. "But in my continued commitment to honesty, I'd rather do the one with less work."

I smiled. "I get that. I really do. But there's something essential about controlling how much money you make. If you can spend $50 to make $100, then you may just be able to spend $100 to make $200. Or $500 to make $1,000. But if you don't have control over the $50—"

"Then it's just random," she said. "You can't control it or make it happen again."

"Exactly. If you can set up any type of marketing, like Amazon ads, that regularly returns a profit, you have a better chance of making it happen twice."

Erin seemed to get it, though telling people they have to keep doing the work isn't exactly like giving them a winning lottery ticket.

"So, there's no skipping this. Keep making ads until I die," she said. "And there really aren't any hidden shortcuts you're keeping from me?"

I shrugged. "You could try to rush by bidding higher. Or messing with the settings. But that just means you're going to lose money with every click. And I really don't want you to stop your success before it even starts."

She ran her fingers through her hair and placed her hands on her neck. "Fine. I'll just ignore the ticking time bomb over my head and figure out a way to stay patient. I'm sorry to say, but that sounds almost as fun as a root canal."

* * *

When you're first starting out with ads, the waiting game is one of the most challenging parts of the process. This is especially true if you're in Erin's situation of not seeing an immediate return. Authors (and really all human people) have the tendency to take action when things aren't working quickly enough. But book marketing isn't something you can force to go faster. Sometimes you have to put in the work and stay optimistic enough that your efforts will eventually pay off.

Pretty much everyone who runs ads wants to quit at a certain point, but if you want to take control over your sales (rather than just letting them happen), you'll have to stay in the game. If you're willing to stick it out, then there are three rules to keep in mind for continuing your Amazon Advertising.

1. Keep Up Your Ad Creation Schedule

When you get motivated by an event or a class, it's easy to start a new habit. But when the memory and the motivation of the webinar or challenge fade, it's very difficult to make that habit consistent. The most important regular task for the successful author advertiser is to create 5-10 new campaigns each week.

Once you've studied and begun to master keyword research (see our earlier chapter on how to conduct this research), it's only moderately difficult to find 500 to 1,000 new keywords. The most challenging part of this task is to avoid it getting crowded out by other urgent tasks on your to-do list. If you lock in your research and ad creation days as a weekly occurrence, then you'll be less likely to forget or ignore them.

Just like a successful writing habit, you'll want to do these tasks at the same time each week. You may even have a location in your house or at the coffee shop that's your "keyword hunting" or "ad making" space. The more you can reenforce this routine, the better.

Don't focus on your stats at this time or closing down ads that haven't done anything yet. Keep your attention on making more ads each and every week.

2. Celebrate the Small Wins

We absolutely want to see tracked sales show up on our Amazon ads dashboard. We also want to see our royalties shoot up to brand new heights on our KDP Reports Dashboard. These are both goals you'll want to keep in mind when you start advertising. But before these two things occur, we need to look for and celebrate the tiniest of victories that will serve as stepping stones to our ultimate goal.

Here are a few smaller wins worth raising a glass to:

- Getting impressions on an ad that previously wasn't doing anything

- Getting your first click on an ad that previously had zero

- Seeing royalties come in for a book that rarely sells (even if it's just a few pennies)

- Improved sales rank on a Kindle Unlimited title which may indicate a new borrow

These achievements may not seem parade-worthy, but it's a good idea to reset your expectations to the above wins. The hope is that you'll eventually get more profit, but skipping too many steps makes you more likely to tumble. Let's get excited about the smaller triumphs first on our way to potentially larger gains in the future.

3. Keep on Writing the Next Book

If you're in the incredibly fortunate position of having a deep backlist of profitable titles, then running ads for the first time could make a huge difference right away. For those who don't, it's worth remembering that Amazon ads are a slow and steady burn. In the midst of learning this evergreen marketing tactic, you'll still want to keep producing more and more books.

The ideal result from ads over the long haul is something I like to call the *profit staircase*. This is when you see a graph of your royalties and the numbers rise each successive month (like a set of stairs). For instance, going from $50 one month to $100 the next and $150 on the third month.

While ads can raise both the floor and ceiling of your earnings, it's important to continue to write books and incorporate other marketing as well. Perhaps to get to that $50 mark in royalties, it was the initial burst of your ads. Getting to $100 in month two might come from ads plus running a temporary discount on your series starter (more on this in a later chapter). And then reaching $150 in the third month might come from the ads plus the launch of the next book in your series.

But we can only layer these ads on top of promos and launches if you continue to put out more books. Getting into that steady writing routine where you're consistently working on the next book will help you to get out of the plateau phase a whole lot sooner.

If you only have one book right now, then do not lose hope. Writing is like a muscle and the more you work it, the easier it will become to complete the publishing process all over again. That being said, I've seen authors with only a handful of books significantly increase their profits from running ads. So, it's still possible to make this work even if you aren't swimming in stories.

Now, it's important to remember that everyone's time frame is different with these ads. You could be making about the same amount you were before running campaigns for a month. It could be three months or even longer. But if you continue to create ads, run promos, and launch new books, then you are a lot more likely to see your breakthrough moment than you were with no ads whatsoever.

Caz Woolley was at the start of becoming a prolific author when she stumbled upon Amazon ads through one of our free challenges. She was already well on her way to writing dozens of books, but she didn't have much traffic to speak of. Nobody was seeing her books, which is why she was earning around $20 a month in royalties.

Creating your first set of ads can be difficult, but Caz did more than dip her toe in the shallow end. She went all in with the low-bid strategy and created campaigns every single week for all of her series starters.

Each month, she created more ads to her series entry points and saw her royalties rise. First, she crossed the $100 mark. As she continued to write more books and make more ads, she reached her first $1,000 month in six-months' time. Within a year, she was earning over $5,000 a month with Amazon ads serving as the primary traffic driver.

In 2021, Caz reached over $150,000 in royalties and shows no signs of stopping. Sometimes, the books are ready to take off but need time and a push from low-cost ads to get going.

In the exercises for this chapter, let's figure out some ways to get excited about keeping your routine going.

* * *

Chapter 7 Exercises

1. What's a small treat or reward you could give yourself for setting up your 5-10 ads this week? Write it down and put it on your calendar for Friday.

2. What's something a little larger you could reward yourself with after completing four straight weeks of ad creation? Put this in the calendar 30 days from now.

3. How would you like to celebrate your first "small win" from your ads when it occurs? Leave yourself a note for some time in the future with your party plan.

4. Do you have a reward for meeting some of your writing and word count goals? If not, what are a few things you could do to incentivize your continued creative output?

* * *

Erin seemed somehow lighter at our next meeting. I imagined that sharing a bit of her burden with me had helped her not feel like she was keeping a secret. But there was another reason I couldn't help but notice as well.

"The ads are actually working," she said. "There are sales happening. And pages read. I suppose you weren't completely making this up as you went along."

I chuckled. "Don't sound so surprised. Ads don't work this quickly for everyone. But it helps that you have a few different series to test things on."

As she flipped through her campaigns, I did some quick calculations in my head.

"I've got to admit, Guru, this stuff was hard at first but I'm actually getting a little bit inspired," she said. "I came up with an idea for a new sci-fi trilogy and my brain had been bone dry for months."

"Uh-huh."

She cleared her throat. "I have kids, so I can tell when someone's not paying attention."

I gritted my teeth. "Sorry about that. I was just doing some math here."

"If you're about to rain on my parade—"

"No. Well, not completely," I said. "It's honestly mostly good news."

Erin folded her arms and looked off to the side. "Just when I get excited about this stuff, you go and kill my buzz. Go ahead and tell me what the issue is."

"I'm really glad the ads have inspired you to write, but I'm not so sure it should be sci-fi."

"What do you mean?" she asked.

I highlighted a few numbers in our shared document. "Your ads are profitable overall, but that doesn't mean all of your books are performing equally."

She sighed. "Which means?"

"It actually might be the sci-fi books that are holding you back from success."

CHAPTER 8

WHAT IF AMAZON ADS JUST DON'T WORK FOR MY BOOK?

"I mean, tell me I'm reading the ads wrong," Erin said. "Because I kind of hope I am."

As I scanned through her stats, I thought about how an author's personality often influenced how they looked at ads and their books in general. An optimistic person would look for any sign of promise with their book marketing. Some kind of reason why their efforts might be working. But a person on the other side of the coin...

"It says here that your romance royalties are $75, and your ad spend is $30, so you're at a $45 profit so far this month," I said. "And the sci-fi—"

"$25 in and $40 out," she said. "And the nonfiction is break even. Somehow with my tired, unwilling brain, you taught me well enough to know when it's not working."

She had the numbers right. Now, I had to see if I could help her spot the gold in her data that she continued to overlook.

"I wish I could say that ads are going to automatically make every book a success. Some books will profit and some won't," I said. "And it all comes down to that book's conversion rate."

She squinted. "I thought profit was the main thing we had to consider."

"If profit is peanut butter, then conversion rate is jelly. They're better together. And when you don't have one," I said. "It may be because of the other."

Erin looked her numbers up and down.

"But the sci-fi has great reviews. I think the cover is pretty good," she said. "Why aren't people buying it as much as the romance?"

I double checked the numbers and saw that readers were buying her romance novel or reading it cover-to-cover on Kindle Unlimited once out of every four clicks. But the conversion rate was three times worse for the sci-fi book, with only one buyer every 12 clicks. There was an obvious winner here, but it seemed like Erin had her money on another horse.

"Let me tell you what I see from the numbers perspective," I said. "The romance series starter is profitable right off the bat. Once you factor in read-through to the next title, that profitability might grow. And if you have good profit and conversion, there's a better chance it'll hold up whether you spend $10 or $100."

She nodded as I continued.

"Meanwhile, the sci-fi is losing you money. Every dollar you spend on the romance might get you two dollars in return," I said. "But that's not the case with the sci-fi."

"As a kid, my parents bought me Barbie and Ken dolls. But I kept stealing my brother's Star Wars action figures instead," she said. "I have sci-fi in my blood. Is the data telling me that I'm wrong?"

I shook my head.

"Of course not. The data is a snapshot in time. Right at this moment in time, you've tapped into something with your romance that's getting sales. Maybe you can eventually make that happen with your sci-fi, too. But also, at this moment in time, you and your family are going through something incredibly challenging," I said. "So, what you do next really depends on your top priority. What's yours?"

Erin looked back at the closed door to her office. I thought about how you can always lock the door, but you can never really block out the circumstances on the other side.

"My priority is not ending up in the poorhouse," she said.

"In that case, let's keep running more ads to what's working."

* * *

In our story example, Erin had one out of three of her books/series that was profitable. Not everyone reading this book is going to be in the same situation. You may write in only one genre and have one series that's profitable. You may write in one genre and have a series that's not profitable.

It's a fortunate thing to have a book that's profitable right out of the box with no additional tweaking. But what do you do if you're in the situation where your book is not currently profitable?

Erin actually took one of the options when she started writing in a different genre. I've seen multiple authors have their "overnight success" after writing their second or third series. All of the wisdom they gained from their initial books proved very lucrative when applied to a "write to market" strategy (see Chris Fox's stellar book *Write to Market* for more details on that strategy).

But if you don't want to write in a new genre, there's another option for what you can do with your existing books to strengthen their chances of profitability. You can do the research and take your time to improve the sales pages of those books.

The sales page is the website on Amazon (or on the other retailers) where readers can purchase your book. If your target readers are buying your title, then it's at least in part because your cover, title, subtitle, book description, price, and look inside are optimized for purchase. If readers aren't buying, then there's a disconnect in one or multiple areas that's causing them to click away.

So, how do you determine if your book needs a marketing makeover?

Let's go over the five-step process.

1. Get 100 Clicks for One Book

When a book isn't initially profitable from Amazon ads, you may be surprised that I don't recommend you turn the ads off. "Why on Earth would you keep them going if I'm bleeding money?" This is because you need to spend a little bit more cash to figure out some essential data about your book.

In the early days of Amazon ads, data nerd and hilarious speaker Brian Meeks was the first self-publishing teacher to help us understand the math. He suggested we needed a certain number of clicks before we could get a big enough sample size and accurately determine our book's potential. His initial recommendation was that you get 1,000 clicks on a single book.

But when I tested my own ads, I realized that 1,000 clicks were far too many for most authors to expect. So, for our own recommendation, we say you should get 100 clicks for the book that you're testing.

This means that if you're running 10 ads and they each get 10 clicks (10 x 10), then you'll have a good enough sample size to test your book's conversion rate.

Even if your book is losing money, this calculation is going to be essential for seeing the "before" picture of your profit potential. The "after" will come once we make our sales page tweaks.

To make your life easier, we recommend collecting this info on a spreadsheet in Excel, Google Sheets, or Numbers. Doing that will spare you from having to go hunting for a sticky note later on.

Note: If you're running other ads like Facebook or BookBub ads, then you'll want to include those clicks in your figures as well.

2. Check Your Sales and Full KU Reads

By collecting your total clicks for one book, you've gathered one part of the equation. The other figures you'll need come from the number of orders and cover-to-cover KU reads on the KDP Reports Dashboard.

Although there are orders and KENP columns on your Amazon ad dashboard, we recommend gathering your info from the KDP Reports Dashboard since it is more accurate with total sales. We combine ebooks and paperback sales for the total number of orders.

If you are in KU, you will also need to go to the Promote & Advertise page on your KDP Bookshelf to find out what your KENPC total is to calculate the equivalent borrows.

For example, if you have 4 ebook orders of your book and 2 paperbacks during the same time period you received the 100 clicks, you'd include those 6 sales as part of your total.

Likewise, if you had 2,000 KU pages read (and your book's KENPC total was 500 pages), then you'd divide 2,000 by 500 to get 4 full KU reads.

You'd then add the 6 orders to those 4 full KU reads to get 10 total sales and full KU reads. We'll call these combined sales figures the Total Units.

Remember, it's important to double check that you're looking at the exact same time period on both the ad dashboard and the KDP Reports Dashboard. If you fail to do this, then you won't be collecting the right kind of data to determine your book's potential for profitability.

3. Divide the Number of Clicks by the Number of Sales/Reads

Now, we complete the essential math problem of dividing the total number of clicks for your book by the total number of units. Doing that will tell us how many readers viewing our sales page it takes for us to actually get one to make the all-important purchase.

In our previous example, we mentioned 6 orders and 4 full KU reads, which gave us 10 total sales and reads that we call units.

If you had 50 clicks from your ads, you'd divide 50 clicks by the 10 units to get a conversion rate of 5 clicks per unit sold.

Remember, you want to use all of the clicks on the same book, but they can be accumulated from multiple ads. Don't include ads for other books in your calculations, even if they are part of the same series. We only want relevant data for the single book we're calculating.

Aside from profit, figuring out this conversion rate statistic will unlock some pretty key information about your book and series' chances for success.

It's worth mentioning here that this is a different way of calculating your book's conversion rate than a handful of teachers might advise. Some authors continue to use only the stats on the ad dashboard to determine if a book is converting well, but we always recommend that you use the split screen method by gathering your sales and royalties data from the KDP Reports page and your clicks data from the ad dashboard.

This goes back to the philosophy I mentioned back in Chapter Four. Since adopting the mindset that all book sales are at least somewhat influenced by the ads we're running, I've seen my own royalties and profits jump. The success stories we've mentioned throughout the book have discovered the same thing and continue to use the conversion rate formula I've mentioned above.

We suggest that you adopt the same point of view with your ad and sales tracking as well.

4. Evaluate Your Results

What does the conversion rate figure we calculated in Step 3 actually tell us?

Some books can be profitable with a worse conversion rate (taking more clicks to register a sale) and others need an extremely strong rate to profit.

For a Book 1 in a series we aim for a conversion rate of 8 clicks for each unit sold.

A standalone book might be able to achieve profitability with 6 clicks per unit.

A 20-page children's book in Kindle Unlimited might require a conversion rate of 3 clicks per unit to be profitable (on account of a full-read only yielding about $0.10 for very short books).

There's no one number to rule them all here, but what do numbers higher than 8:1 mean for your book?

If your book has a conversion rate of 9 or 10 to 1, then you may be able to sneak in a profit with a long enough series.

If it's in the 11 to 15:1 range, a small tweak or two of your sales page might help bring you into profitability.

If takes 15 clicks or more to sell a book, then you may need to make more drastic changes such as a new cover, blurb, title, etc.

It's tough to spend time collecting 100 clicks for a book only to find out that it's running into trouble making sales. However, it's better to find out sooner rather than later.

At 39 cents per click, it would take a grand total of $39 to pay for 100 clicks. It's a small price to pay to get the data you need to set your book up for future success. Spending that money on ads now and learning whether or not you need a sales page tweak will save you years of stumbling around in the dark. It comes down to whether you'd rather know if there's a problem or if you'd prefer to remain oblivious for the foreseeable future.

If you can make some changes in the next month or two that might bring your beloved book into profitability in the future, then it's worth finding out the truth about where your book sits on Amazon.

While it's tempting to rush into making changes on your book's sales page, we don't recommend you change anything until after you've completed Steps 1-4 first.

5. Make One or More Tweaks and Re-test

Do you fondly remember your high school science class? Yeah, me neither.

But when you ran experiments back in those halcyon days, you would set up a control group and an experiment group. The control was established to see how things behaved under normal circumstances. This allowed you to compare the regular way things work to the unknown experiment group.

Step 4 allowed us to collect the data we needed to define our control group (how our book performs with nothing changed). Here in Step 5, we need to set up our experiment group by making one or more changes to our sales page.

There are easier tweaks to make to your book's price, subtitle, and the first line of your book description. There are also harder changes to make like your book's Look Inside sample, blurb, cover, or title.

If your book is converting at 8 clicks per sale or better (i.e. 6:1 or 3:1), then you can skip this step. But if you're not seeing a profit or a low enough conversion rate, then one or more of these changes may be needed.

The goal is to bring the elements of your sales page more in line with what readers expect in your genre. For instance, if you write sci-fi space opera and you don't have a spaceship on the front cover, then your book may not look enough like space opera for readers of that genre to make a purchase.

Once you've made the changes, you'll want to repeat Step 1 to collect an additional 100 clicks on your book. This is the part too many authors skip because they just want to assume the issue will now be solved. But when you don't know if the changes you've made have been successful or not, then you still need to collect data on the profit and conversion for your tweaked book.

The bottom line is that if you have one book that's profiting and one book that isn't, you've got books in two separate camps. The profitable book (let's call it Book A) is fair game to keep running profitable, low bid ads to.

Book B, on the other hand, has now become part of an experiment. And once you've collected 100 clicks on it, you'll want to tweak the sales page, and get an additional 100 clicks to see if its fate has changed.

Ayden K. Morgen was in a bit of a pickle with her Amazon ads. She'd found some success and reached over $1,000 a month from the titles she ran campaigns to. There was only one problem: some of her books were rejected for ads because of the raciness of the covers and a few of the words found in the titles.

When Ayden published the books, she was simply following the industry trends, but hadn't realized some of that cover and title advice restricted her from ads. She had a choice to make: keep the covers that "everybody said" would sell or change them so she could run ads. Ayden chose the latter, which took time, effort, and energy. Through her patience and dedication to marketing her books in a way that would let her run ads, Ayden got her campaigns approved and saw her income rise to over $10,000 a month within 8 months.

I recently connected with her and found that she'd even hit a $200,000 year by continuing to market her books in a way that would let her run ads. Sometimes, when Amazon ads aren't profitable or working for your books, you need to change the books to allow them to succeed.

You are under no obligation to advertise a profitable book and run a conversion rate experiment at the same time. It's all a matter of the time, energy, and money you have available to spend. And when you have a book or series that can already make you money, it makes a whole lot of sense to continue focusing on the book that works.

* * *

Chapter 8 Exercises

1. Create a new spreadsheet document. Add column headers for *Name of Book*, *Likely Profitable* and *Likely Needs Work*.

2. Put your series starters or standalone into one column or the other based on your best guess.

3. If you have 100 ad clicks for any of the titles, run the numbers for your books to see if you were right.

4. If you had to guess, what sales page element of your *Likely Needs Work* books would be the top priority for you to change? Make note of that in your document.

* * *

Erin seemed to get the idea of conversion rate right away. When she ran the numbers on her own, the idea that her romance was profitable while her other books weren't sunk in like a sponge. She created more ads for the romance book and even began writing a new book in that series.

"Did you see that I had a $40 day?" she asked. "I'm not sure I've ever had a day that high. Even when I was pouring money down the drain for a dollar a click."

"I did notice that. Congratulations!" I said. "How does that make you feel?"

Her shoulders seemed to slump at the question. "Fair to middling. I mean, extremely grateful, of course."

I knew right then and there that it wasn't Erin the Publisher having that reaction. It wasn't Erin the Parent or Erin the Wife. It was Erin the Artist.

"I'm not sensing too much excitement over your highest royalty day ever," I said.

She groaned. "I know. I'm terrible. But something about it doesn't feel right."

"You don't have to force yourself to write more romance, you know."

She shook her head. "I do, though. It might be my family's best shot right now. But it makes me feel like an absolute fraud."

Impostor syndrome was a terrible thing. "You're not. You're an author."

"Yeah," she glumly replied. "An author who may never have fun again."

CHAPTER 9
WHAT IF I DON'T LIKE WHAT THE AD DATA TELLS ME?

I was hesitant to intrude into Erin's distressing thought process. I'd worked with plenty of authors who'd run into stress with the numbers. She had it better than some, but I knew that telling her that wouldn't necessarily quell her fear.

"If it's all about the money, that's fine," she said with resignation. "I mean, plenty of people spend all day in a cubicle for 30 years for a company they don't care about. Right?"

"Is that what primarily writing romance would be like for you?" I asked.

She huffed. "You think I'm being unreasonable, don't you?"

I put up my hands. "I didn't say anything like that. I just want to understand."

"Of course, writing any books would be better than working a day job I hate. But none of this is going according to my plan," she said. "I thought I would live out my dreams writing the next Star Wars and geeking out with my fans. But running ads and writing about shirtless guys was never part of my dream. I just wanted to try something different. I didn't want to lock myself in for life."

I nodded. "I understand. It's really hard to ignore when the masses have spoken. And maybe the sci-fi will still factor in down the line. Maybe it won't. But a lot of authors struggle with trying to be an artist and an entrepreneur at the same time."

"An artist?" She snorted. "You make it sound so pompous."

"I don't think that at all. But at some point, you may have to make a trade off. I think it was John Cusack who once said, 'I do one project for them, and I do one project for me.' Maybe romance is your 'one for them' project."

There was a long silence as she digested my thoughts. When she spoke again, her voice was quieter than normal. "But what if I get stuck doing projects that are just for them?"

Rather than answering her question, I posed another one to her. "What is it you like about writing sci-fi?"

"I don't know." She shrugged. "Exploring new worlds? Captains trying to do what's right against incredible odds?"

I let the details roll around in my head before making a suggestion. "Well, maybe there's a way to bring some of that into your romance novels. Different countries instead of different planets? Characters in love trying to do what's right... but on Earth?"

"I'm putting up every last wall of resistance to stop this from happening, aren't I?" She sighed. "Bryan, I'm absolutely terrified about all of this."

Her admission hung in the air. I felt the urge to give her a hug through the Zoom.

"This stuff is all really scary. Paying money to Amazon to run ads. Not knowing for sure if the data is telling the truth. Taking a different path than you planned," I said. "Being afraid is pretty normal."

She leaned forward on her desk as if the chair could no longer support her weight. "How many people give up at this point? When they don't like the numbers, how many people just ignore them?"

"Out of the ones who test their profitability and conversion, I'd say more than half quit at that point. When they don't like the answer, they continue asking the same questions over and over until they get the answer they want."

"That makes a lot of sense," she said. "Ugh, this is so stressful."

"So, are you going to be one of them?" I asked.

"One of who?"

I took a deep breath. "Are you going to be one of the authors who gives up?"

* * *

Of the tens of thousands of authors we've had the pleasure of working with, the Amazon ads data has revealed a lot of harsh truths. Erin's situation is better than some, as she actually has a series with the potential for profit. And there's always the chance that her other genres would have better luck with improved sales pages.

But unfortunately, not all authors are in that boat. The initial assessment after 30-60 days' worth of ads or 100 clicks can clearly indicate your next best step as an author. That doesn't mean you're going to want to listen to what the info has to say.

When I see an author stare their next actions in the face and take a courageous step forward, it's incredibly rewarding to me and my team. Part of the work they do is more than ad creation and conversion tracking. A huge part of it is dealing with difficult situations and the anxiety that results.

Here are a few situations you might be in after checking the data and what you could consider doing next.

1. No Profit from Any Books

Let's say that you've run ads for 2-3 months and you've gotten 50-100 clicks on each of your books. And once you've broken down the numbers, you've found that Book A lost $10, Book B lost $20, and

Book C lost $30. Overall, that puts you down $60 with zero candidates for profitability.

After you take a few deep breaths, here's what we'd recommend. First, give your books a little more time to see if sales of later books in the series lead to profitability. You could lose money on the first book in the Book A series and then make it up on sales of the rest of the titles.

If your patient waiting game did not yield profitability, then you'll want to look for any obvious sales page deficits that could be reducing conversion (see Chapter 8 for potential tweaks). Don't see any easy fixes? You might need to get a new cover, title, subtitle, blurb, and rework the Look Inside preview.

Nobody likes to hear that they may have to spend more money on the sales page when they've already plunked down several hundred bucks to produce their book. But if you're committed to making one of your series profitable in the long run, then this may be your next best step.

If you've been writing in an existing universe for a while, your best work may be four or five books deep (where new readers won't see your improvement in skill). But when you take on a new series, readers will experience your growth as an author right from the series starter. I've seen this path lead to great success for multiple authors.

You could also cut your losses by extensively researching a new genre to write in, and start penning a radically different series under a second pen name.

The majority of authors running into these profitability problems ignore them and keep advertising the same book no matter what the numbers say. Doing what you've always done will likely lead to the same results, so it's usually a more profitable course to make some kind of change.

2. Profit from One Book/Series But Not All

This is pretty close to the situation described with Erin, where one book or series is actually making money. And while we'd love to have all of our books returning some profit back to us, it's not a bad place to be to have one thing working. The most important thing here is to recognize the situation and take action.

Once you've gotten those 50-100 clicks on each of your series starters or standalone, you'll still want to look at that profit and conversion data. There may be one clear winner as in Erin's case or a couple that are yielding more royalties than the money you've spent on ads. After you've collected the info, it's a good idea to temporarily pause the ads on the books that are losing money.

Are these books a lost cause because you can't run profitable ads to them? Not necessarily, as you may be able to make some sales page changes to the books that help improve your chances at profit. But while you ponder what improvements to make, you can set these ads aside while you focus your attentions on the healthier titles.

How do you give that book or series your attention? The best way to give it that focus is to keep creating those 5-10 ads per week to that title. We don't recommend making tweaks to the sales pages for the profitable titles "to try to make them better" because we don't know if our changes will make things worse. I once had an author ask for new book descriptions for a series that was yielding a sale every 2.5 clicks and a significant profit.

As the saying goes, if it ain't broke, don't fix it.

It can be frustrating when you've written multiple books and only one or a couple of them earn money. But it's important to remember that you're running a business and even the biggest companies in the world have "lower earners" in their product lines. After all, we're not using Apple Newton tablets and Google Glass eyewear. But once those companies realized these products weren't as popular, they focused their advertising on the products that would lead to profit because that's where the money is.

Follow the lead of Apple and Google by advertising the books that give you the best chance for future success.

3. Profit, But Not Enough to Live On

The ideal situation is that most or all of your books and series are actually profitable and it's enough to give you a full-time earning. I'm not going to break that out into a separate situation here because the solution is to keep running ads to your profitable books. I've seen authors in this scenario climb to $10k per month and even $100k per month by continuing to run ads to books that "print money."

But what if you're a step down from that? What if you actually have profitable books and ads, but the profit isn't anywhere close to your goals?

The first thing to do is keep running ads to the books that are making you money. Even $1 in profit is better than no profit at all.

Secondly, it's important to be patient. Amazon ads remain a slow burn and if you keep running more ads and writing more books, then that profit number will often start to grow. A $20 profit month can build to a $50 profit second month and a $75 profit third month.

But you probably didn't get into this business of self-publishing with just $75 a month in mind. At this point in your career, you may have to ask yourself the tough questions. You may need to decide if the next book or books you intend to write will give you the best shot at future success. There's even a chance you may have to learn additional skills like writing powerful prose and market research expertise.

I recently held a panel with three six-figure authors who have used Amazon ads to jumpstart their careers. One of the authors, Trixie Silvertale, mentioned something that stuck with me.

"You have to avoid taking anything in publishing personally," she said. "Because if someone who knows what they're talking about says you're doing something wrong, then it's a good idea to listen."

Trixie related the story of an experienced beta reader tearing her series starter apart because it wasn't hitting the genre tropes. Instead of sulking about the feedback, Trixie hired this honest beta reader as a virtual assistant. The notes helped inform the start of a very popular 19-book series that took her career to a whole new level.

If you have goals of reaching a certain profit amount and the genres you've written in aren't getting you closer to that milestone, then it may not make sense to continue writing that series or genre.

Like I said, these are going to be tough (perhaps even brutal) questions, but they are the ones you need to face in order to succeed in the challenging self-publishing world.

When you've collected at least one month's worth of clicks, spend, and royalties data, those numbers will tell you where you stand. You absolutely have the freedom to ignore what the data tells you, but in my professional opinion, you probably shouldn't.

Emily Childs considered herself a "shiny object gal" and had multiple series to her name she wanted to get selling. While a newer series was slightly profitable, she found that an older series she'd let die had a slightly better conversion rate. Emily looked deeper into the market trends of her older series using resources like K-Lytics and reading in the genre. She was shocked to find that the subgenre now had a new cover style and she rushed out to rebrand and reblurb the series in question.

Emily could've ignored the numbers and kept on moving forward with the newer series. She could've let her production schedule get in the way of her profit. But when she pivoted her plan to follow the ad data, she blasted through her previous royalties goals. First, she passed $2,500 a month. Then $5,000. Eventually, she reached a whopping $20,000+ per month and it all started with a deep look at the data.

Sometimes, listening to the ad data can help you blast through the current ceiling to your publishing profit.

* * *

Chapter 9 Exercises

1. Currently, what would you say the data of your previous advertising and publishing is telling you?

2. Since it's too early to make a call based on this info, write down when you plan to create your 5 -10 Amazon ads this week.

3. Have you ever considered enhancing your writing or market research skills? What would be your next step for building those craft and marketing muscles?

4. On a scale of 1 to 10, with 1 being never and 10 being always, how willing are you to admit when you're wrong about something? How willing are you to accept feedback?

* * *

"Just to make sure I'm understanding the truth bomb here. You're telling me that some of the things I've written aren't selling?" Erin asked. "And it'd take some serious work to hammer them into shape?"

"Mm-hmm," I replied.

"But, I do have at least one series and genre that's selling and earning me a pretty decent profit," she said. "At least that's what it seems like the data is telling me."

I nodded. "I agree."

She folded her arms. "And you're asking me if I'm going to listen to what the numbers say or just keep doing the things I've always done that have never worked? Essentially giving up in the process?"

"That's the big question."

"Guru, I'm tired of things not working. You've actually shown me something that does work. I'm not giving up. As much as it hurts, I'm going to keep moving forward," she said. "Please, don't gloat too much."

I tried to keep my smile at bay. "I would never," I said. "I'm proud that you've decided to keep moving forward on your journey."

As always, the next couple of months were a whirlwind.

Erin kept me posted with her numbers and her writing progress. She postponed the sci-fi book as the next project on her docket and pivoted to a romance trilogy set in small but exotic locales. Her profit grew from month to month while she continued to create ads for her best-selling titles.

By the third month since she'd made the commitment, she reached over $750 in royalties and over $500 in profit.

"The hubby's had a lot of interviews but no bites," Erin said at our next meeting. "But thanks to the extra profit, it looks like we'll be able to stretch the savings further than we thought!"

"That's fantastic news. And congrats on the launch last week," I said. "Seems like things are really heading in a great direction. You've done some amazing work here!"

Erin rolled her eyes. "You're seriously not going to toot your own horn here?" She laughed when I shook my head. "Well, toot toot. This wouldn't have happened without you being so, so annoying."

"I will take that as a compliment," I said. "But we can't rest on our laurels. We've got bigger fish to fry."

"You think my fish can cook even better?" she asked.

"Absolutely. You just hit $500 a month in profit. In addition to having a celebration about your accomplishments, it means that it's finally time to start scaling up."

CHAPTER 10

HOW DO I KNOW WHAT'S WORKING WITH MY ADS AND HOW DO I SCALE IT UP?

Erin rubbed her hands together. "I knew you were holding back some secrets from me. Now, can I *finally* switch back to those $1 bids?"

I shook my head. "No, it's rare that we'll ever use bids that high. First, we need to make sure your series is fully optimized before we scale up."

"Guru, has anyone told you that you're pretty much the Fun Police?" she asked. "Besides, the conversion rate already told us my book was optimized. What else do I need to know?"

I was glad to see Erin had been paying full attention.

"To my knowledge, I've always been a party pooper. And you're right, the book is in pretty good shape. However, what about the rest of the books in the series?"

She stared me down through the monitor. "What about them?"

"We want to make sure you're sending as many readers to Book 2 as possible," I said. "Let me flip to the back of your first romance book."

As I scrolled, Erin protested. "Every time I want to break out the champagne, you tell me there's another thing to tweak. What does the back of my book have to do with ads, anyway?"

"Just a second," I said. "There. Read me what it says in your back matter, right after your book finishes."

"Coming in June 2021. Pre-order your copy of Book 2 in the series." Erin cringed since we were well past June 2021. "Oh no. I even forgot to put an actual link. Now, I feel stupid."

"There's no reason to feel bad. I can promise that you are not the only person who's done this. Plenty of authors forget to update their back matter after publication," I said. "But if you do, you may not get as many folks reading through to the next book, which could make your ads less profitable."

Erin put up her hands. "You know, before, I would've let this ruin my day. But I'd rather fix this now and move on with my life."

"And once you do," I said, "you can do something fancy we haven't learned yet."

"Something fancy? Okay, I'm listening."

I maneuvered over to her ads dashboard and clicked into an auto ad with dozens of clicks and a few tracked sales. "We're going to use the data here to make what we call a second generation ad. See this keyword for the book *The Ceiling of Love*? You've gotten three tracked sales from readers searching for it."

Erin leaned in closer to study the numbers. "I've never even heard of that book. So, should I raise the bid? Or put it into its own ad?"

"Not quite. Let's head over to Amazon and check out what's in this book's also-boughts," I said as I scrolled to the bottom of the page. "We know that this book is a winner, so we're going to guess that folks who bought books in tandem with it will like yours, too."

Erin smiled. "So, these are new keywords I may not have even tried. And you're going to put those into an ad, aren't you?"

"Yes, ma'am. When we do these ads based on the keywords that have worked to this point, we call them 'second generation' ads."

"Is that the big change?" she asked. "Do I just do second gen ads and that'll scale everything up?"

"You're still going to mostly do ads based on your own research," I said. "But now you can sprinkle a couple of second gen ads in every month or so."

She sighed. "I'm still stuck making 5-10 new ads per week, then, huh?"

"It's all in how you look at it, right? You don't *have* to make ads every week. You *get* to make ads every week." I tried to reason with her. "You're making more money now, so what's the rush?"

"The ticking clock looming over my head. All my savings running out," she said. "I feel like I'm out of time."

The slow and steady Amazon ad philosophy comes with plenty of mental landmines. The idea of scaling with care was definitely one of them.

"If we go too fast on this, we may eat up all of our profits on not nearly enough data," I said. "It may not be flashy or exciting, but keeping our habits going while making a few scaling tests is one of the best ways to earn more royalties for less ad spend."

"Everything in my brain is telling me to rush." She sighed in resignation. "But I can't afford to screw this up, so fine, we'll do it your way. Tell me exactly what I need to do."

* * *

Here's where we get into the portion of the book that won't apply to some authors.

Scaling up your ads, a.k.a. trying to increase your ad spend and royalties while maintaining the same percentage of profit, really only makes sense if you're already earning a profit. I've seen some authors try their hand at the strategies from Chapters 1-9 a few times until they finally made it work. Strategies like second generation ads or running ads outside of the

U.S. shouldn't be on your agenda until you're earning at least $250 in profit per month.

If you do continue to read without having that amount of profit, then please do it as an exercise of finding out what to expect going forward. The disclaimer has been made!

Scaling is all about continuing to double down on what works. We're not suddenly going to throw in a bunch of different ad types because we can still optimize what we're already trying. Here are a few ways to prepare for and engage in the scaling process.

1. Optimize What You Have

Once you've secured a profit for a book or a series, you may think that you're home free. But there are a few easy tweaks you can do that will almost always help you increase your return on your ad spend.

One of the first ways is exactly what I shared with Erin: improving your back matter. When six-figure author Quinn Ward went from under $1,000 a month to over $10,000 a month in royalties, ads were half of the battle. The other half was all about sending readers exactly where they wanted them to go upon finishing the book.

And the creative control that self-publishing brings you allows you to increase your percentage of how many buyers read through to Books 2 and beyond. First, you need a strong call to action. What's likely to work better?

A. *Here's where you can find Book 2.*

B. *Want to find out if Braedon survives his quest? Click here to start reading Book 2 instantly.*

It's likely that B will help readers who've loved Book 1 know exactly where to go to keep reading the series.

Secondly, you've got to think about placement. Rather than wait until you've shared a note, an excerpt, and an About the Author page, it's a stellar idea to keep this call to action on the same page as the final words of your book.

All you have to do after your novel's final word is put an ornamental break or some asterisks and return carriages before including a linked call to action to the next logical book.

This change alone can get 5-20% more readers to continue your series and add to your book's profitability.

Other things you may want to consider optimizing: the sales page of Book 2, the landing page for any email lists you link to, the clarity of the rest of the back matter, or anything else that might help you earn more profit through series read through.

2. Create 2-3 Second Generation Ads Per Month

Most of the ads you'll create over your life as an author advertiser will be based on your general keyword research. You'll hunt down keywords that you think will work and then put them into ads with 100-150 keywords per campaign. In the grand scheme of your ads, we like to refer to these researched ads as first generation ads.

But once a couple of months have gone by and you've gathered more data, you may have gotten enough clicks and tracked sales to set up 2-3 second generation ads per month.

Second generation ads are when you take a successful keyword like a book title or a search term and you find 100-150 new targets based around that target. If a keyword is relevant to your book and it has either tracked sales or tracked pages read, then it might be a good candidate as the basis for a second gen ad. When you create this new ad, you can reuse the same keyword from your first generation ad and not worry too much about whether or not the two ads compete against one another.

If you don't have any tracked sales or tracked pages read from your ad, then you likely haven't collected enough data to create one of these ad types. It's a better idea to keep creating first generation ads until you've gathered more stats. My advice of patience will continue to apply throughout this process.

With 5-10 new ads recommended per week and only 2-3 second gen ads per month, that still leaves you with 17+ first generation ads that you'll want to keep making. Research will remain the focal point of your ad creation and the majority of your ads will be keyword ads (rather than auto or category).

Now, you may be wondering if this is the time to start using higher bids. We recommend that even at this stage of the game, you try to keep bids below 39 cents for a series starter (34 cents for standalone and 15 cents for children's or low content) to see if you can get traction at this number. There's no sense in paying more than you have to if you're able to get clicks and impressions for less.

In the slow burn of Amazon Advertising, these second generation ads may take a few weeks to really get going with the low bid strategy. But if you keep working to make more relevant ads over time, then you'll generate more clicks and royalties from the right kind of reader.

3. Choose One Additional Ad Territory

Some authors desperately want to advertise outside of the U.S. Before you do, I offer a word of caution. Unless your book has a UK, Australian, or Canadian focus, then your best-selling market will likely be the U.S. This means that most authors will have their best chance of profit running ads solely to the United States.

But let's say you've read my disclaimer and you still want to try it. We recommend you stay in just one territory (and usually only the U.S.) until you're at least making $100 in profit per month. Once you've hit that mark, we suggest expanding to one more territory maximum.

Why shouldn't you run ads to all potential ad territories all at once? First and foremost, they're all on separate ad platforms. That means you'll need to keep track of an entire separate dashboard, graph, and campaign list for each territory you advertise in. Secondly, you will have to deal with different currencies and factor that in with your ad costs. And lastly, some of these territories charge additional taxes on your ad spend, which can eat into your bottom line.

Once you've picked one additional territory, like the UK, you'll want to set up the usual suspects of one auto ad per format, a few category ads, and 5-10 keyword ads per week. At the time of this writing, ads outside of the U.S. do not currently have ad copy, so you won't need to insert any in there.

We recommend starting your bids even lower in international territories than you do in the U.S. Rather than starting at 39 cents, you can often get these ads going for less than 20 cents (or the monetary equivalent of less than 20 cents) as your bid. In some of the territories without as large an audience, you may even be able to find clicks below 15 cents. If you can get impressions and clicks at 15 cents or below, then that's where we'd recommend you start.

As your ads begin to receive clicks, you'll want to check how your profit is doing on a territory-by-territory basis. You may find that you're profitable in the U.S. with a certain book and not-so-profitable in the UK or Australia. This will help you learn if your book has the opportunity for success in more than one territory.

Conversion rate for your book may differ from territory to territory, so don't assume that a book with high profit in the U.S. will automatically have the same results in the U.K.

It's a major commitment to run ads throughout the world, so make sure to only take this on if you're at $100 in profit and if you're able to monitor more than one territory at a time.

I know that many authors reading a book like this will skip to the "scaling" chapter and miss everything that came before it. As much as I love all authors, whether you're a speed scroller or not, I'd suggest reading the entire book from cover to cover to understand our philosophy from start to finish.

I've seen hundreds of authors go from under $50 a month to over $100 a month with ads. We've even been fortunate enough to see dozens going higher than $1,000 a month. None of these results came quickly, as good things take time (and great things take even longer). Keep that in mind as you continue to progress in your advertising journey.

Some authors reading this book might be frustrated that many of the examples I've shared are from popular genres. But author Glenn Salter has found his greatest advertising success with medieval European historical fiction, a subgenre that's rarely on the tip of the book marketing tongue. At first, Glenn struggled to get impressions and clicks on his ads. It would've been easy to assume that there simply weren't enough readers out there for his book.

But Glenn wanted to make sure that no stone was left unturned. He dove deep into the Three Generation System of ads, doubling down on his campaigns by creating ads based around his most profitable keywords. Glenn pushed his ads to the brink by tweaking the budget and even creating a unique scaling method we've dubbed The Salter Slam in his honor. This method involves putting the ads for one book into a portfolio and letting the monthly budget all but run out before adding $1 to $5 to keep the ads humming along.

Glenn worked his ads hard and saw his royalties go up from three-figures to a consistent four-figures, despite his smaller genre. Sometimes, scaling is less about each individual ad and more about how to use the campaigns to scale the book as a whole.

* * *

Chapter 10 Exercises

1. Take a peek at the back of your e-book using your computer or an e-reader.

2. Do you make it easy for readers to immediately go to your next book at the conclusion of your story? If not, put a back matter edit on your to-do list for the next week.

3. What steps do you still need to take before you feel you're ready for second generation ads?

4. How will you set "reasonable" expectations on when it's time to begin scaling your ads?

* * *

Erin began putting the scaling steps into practice. Within weeks of changing her back matter, she saw sales of her second romance book rise. The enhanced read-through plus her new ads in the UK helped her have her second best month ever.

But when our next meeting began and I saw the look on her face, I could tell exactly what had happened.

"It was good while it lasted," she said in defeat. "I guess ads just don't like me anymore."

I took a deep breath and dove into the stats. While her clicks and impressions had dropped since last month, her royalties still remained much higher than usual.

"Is it too early in the morning to remind you that the sky probably isn't falling?" I asked.

Erin didn't seem to hear me. "Clicks are down. Royalties are down."

"But still higher than two months ago," I countered.

"My new ads are hardly doing anything." She threw her hands up in frustration. "I think ads just don't work for me."

As the son and grandson of a trio of teachers, I wondered how often my parents and bubbie had to help a student exit an emotional spiral.

"Facts over feelings, Erin," I gently reminded her. "You just had a $900 month of royalties. A few months ago, you didn't even break $200. When your royalties go up, it probably isn't random."

She sighed in agitation. "Yeah, but why do my royalties have to go up and down like this? Are you sure this isn't the end of the gravy train?"

"Most authors experience normal ups and downs. There are no guarantees here. We have no way of knowing if next month will be $300 or $1,300," I said. "But we do have a few tricks up our sleeves for waking up our slower ads."

"As long as it doesn't involve a ritual sacrifice, I'll do whatever I can to keep this from falling apart."

I nodded. "Don't worry, no shamans required. But in order to make our Amazon ads work better, we may actually need a little bit of extra help from another website entirely."

CHAPTER 11

WHAT DO I DO IF MY ADS SLOW DOWN?

I'd seen what Erin was going through far too many times. Plenty of authors I'd worked with had assumed rising book sales would always go up and that if the opposite occurred there must be something wrong. Unfortunately for Erin and the rest, royalties can fluctuate from month to month. But it's what you do when that happens that can make all the difference.

"Why do you have a contingency plan for ads slowing down?" Erin asked. "If your system works, then the numbers should just keep going up."

"What were your average royalties per month last year?" I asked. "Ballpark estimate."

"Lower than they are now. With less profit," she said. "But I meant they should go up every month."

I nodded. "I wish that was the case. I've been publishing for over a decade now. It's a fact of life that things fluctuate in our industry. Everything from the time of year to world events can impact our book sales. You can't assume each month is going to grow forever."

"I guess that would just be far too easy," Erin grumbled. "Fine. Then what can I do to make this dip temporary?"

"First, let's get in touch with reality." I scrolled through her numbers. "You're projected to make $700 this month instead of $900. That's still way higher than the $200 you had last quarter."

"And that's a normal kind of drop?" she asked.

"Unfortunately, occasional monthly drops like this are typical. But as long as we're trending in the right direction each quarter and half-year, we're on the right track."

She let her eyes drift away from the camera. "You know not having any clue how much money you'll earn each month is totally nerve-wracking, right?"

"I know. It's one of the toughest parts of being an author," I said. "And that's why we have a plan to bump our royalties and our ads back up. Wanna give it a shot?"

She let out an annoyed chuckle. "Fine, Guru. What's our Plan B?"

* * *

I see an interesting trend in self-publishing from time to time. I'll watch an indie author who is consistently complaining about their fluctuating royalties all year long. But when I actually see their stats comparison from year-to-year, they'll have boosted their royalties by a factor of five, ten, or even higher.

Going from $100 to $1,000 or $500 to $5,000 in one year's time is a huge improvement for any small business. Even if we don't reach a full-time income in our "hopeful" projected schedule, we need to celebrate the tiny and medium victories, not just the gigantic ones.

But even if we continue to grow our book sales on a quarterly or yearly basis, there's always a chance of a backslide. After all, more books are published every single day and some ads can grow stale over time. There are also plenty of things that are out of our control like genres sliding in and out of popularity as well as world events that impact the global economy. Fortunately, there are actions you can take on a weekly, monthly, and quarterly basis to wake your ads up and get your royalties and profits back on track.

Note: If you've been running ads for less than two months, then read these ideas for informational purposes. You don't need to wake up an ad within the first month of your campaigns. Our patient primate mascot the Zen Lemur thanks you for waiting.

1. Change the Budget or End Date

Since helping tens of thousands of authors run Amazon ads, we've picked up a few tricks along the way that can help get our low-performing ads moving in the right direction. Two of those tricks have to do with changing how much budget you give your campaign and when your campaign is scheduled to end.

If you've run Amazon ads before, then you know the budget you set for your campaign is often wishful thinking. Using a lower bid like $0.34 for a standalone or $0.39 for a series starter along with a $5 daily budget will likely spend less than $1 per day. Sometimes, when you raise the budget from $5 to $10 or $20, you may start to see more impressions and clicks, but you still likely won't spend more than $1 or $2.

In fact, we've even seen ads with low bids and extremely high budgets like $1,000+ per day spend less than $2. Unlike some other ad platforms like Facebook, you aren't targeting millions to billions of users at once with your auto, category, and keyword ads. The pool of users searching for a certain term or genre is significantly smaller than that, meaning that even a modest budget might not entirely get spent. Add to that the fact that we're trying to bid modestly (and profitably) from the beginning, which keeps costs down and may limit our clicks.

If you have an ad getting fewer than 10 clicks per week, then you can try keeping the bid the same while raising the budget in an effort to get the ad going. Whenever you make a tweak like this, we recommend waiting at least a week until you make any additional changes.

Another technique that requires a little bit of extra attention is the budget slamming technique developed by Quinn Ward. During an attempt to get their ads spending less, they dropped all the campaign budgets to $1. Surprisingly, Quinn's ad spend went up! We surmise that this method starves the ads, in a way, and encourages them to use the small budget they have left.

But once you "slam" an ad, you want to keep an eye on which ads then spend their entire budget in a single day. Because once the ad does eat up the $1, you'll want to slowly but surely increase the budget by no more than a $1 at a time. Because this method requires a greater understanding of the platform, we recommend holding off on it until you've been running ads for at least a month or two.

One additional tweak you can make is to shorten the duration of your campaign. To do this, you can change your end date to be one week or a few days sooner than you had originally. For instance, if your campaign was going to end May 31st, you can change it to May 24th.

Much like the Budget Slamming technique, this seems to "scare" the ad (I know, ads aren't people) into actually spending the budget. I would only recommend this method if you're very good at putting things in your calendar, because it's very easy to forget that you have some ads ending on the 31st and a few ending earlier.

There are those in the author community who oppose this tactic for one reason or another. After testing it out with tens of thousands of authors over the last couple of years, we feel confident in the anecdotal data, but you're always welcome to try and see for yourself.

Experimenting with different budgets and end dates is a quick and painless way to get your older ads working again.

2. Run Discount Promos

The Amazon algorithm works in mysterious ways. Through running thousands of ad campaigns and facilitating authors to create tens of thousands of others, we've detected a few interesting patterns. One of those trends is that when you send other forms of traffic to your books, the impressions and clicks of your ads tend to go up as well.

This means that if you're running Amazon ads to a Book 1 in your series and you send an email out to your mailing list, you may start to see those ads serve better. The same is true if you run paid ads on other platforms like Facebook and BookBub. But before you go out and chase the shiny objects of these other platforms, we recommend an old-school alternative that will help you get more sales, a stronger sales rank, and a significant increase in your ad clicks.

Running stacked discount promos for your book is a technique that's been employed nearly as long as KDP has been around. This strategy sees you temporarily discount your book to $0.99 or free as you work with several services like Bargain Booksy, BookSends, eReaderNewsToday, and others to have multiple days of increased sales from your target readers. While you will earn lower royalties when a book is at a sale price, the number of orders during this time can improve your sales rank and increase your visibility in bestseller lists. But the real trick is the double effect the promotion can have on your Amazon ads.

Even if you don't receive a boost in sales rank, this strategy can still have benefits for your campaigns. The first step of this $0.99 or free sale strategy will often help your ads get more impressions right off the bat. With the lower price point, there's less of a resistance to potential readers clicking through, which tells the Amazon algorithm that your ads should be seen far and wide. Even doing a discount once a quarter can help get your campaigns out of a slump.

The second impact on your ads comes from the marketing services you work with. Each of the above-mentioned sites, along with dozens of others, have an email list of readers who enjoy reading your genre. When you discount your book and pay the fee to have your book advertised with one of these sites, your book may receive hundreds of additional clicks and dozens of sales. When the Amazon algorithm detects this, you'll start to get even more impressions and clicks.

Since ads can tend to die down every 90 days or so, we recommend running this two-pronged discount strategy once per quarter for each series starter or box set.

Let's say you have two series. You could run a free promotion for a series starter for Series A in January and a $0.99 promo for the box set for Series B in February.

The following quarter starting in April, you can do another promotion for Series A (perhaps this time at $0.99) and a free promo for the series starter of Series B in May. If you have three series, then you could effectively have a promotion every single month of the year.

Now, it's important to remember that you only want to do this with series that are profitable through 90+ days' worth of info. It's also worth noting that these promotions will mess with your data and potentially lead to a lower-than-normal read-through percentage (especially with free promotions). Readers who purchase primarily 99 cent or free books may not be as likely to buy a second book in your series as a reader who often orders full-priced books. This means that if your read-through percentage is usually 50%, shortly after a promotion it may be closer to 30% while these "discount readers" finish the first book.

Shortly after a discount promotion when your read-through is lower than normal isn't a time we would recommend you use for determining conversion rate or read-through. In fact, we often refer to this data as "dirty," which means it's going to be different than the normal numbers you'd receive. We suggest waiting 30 days after a promotion to begin collecting clean conversion and read-through data.

As long as you understand the data during this time will be a bit "dirty," this shouldn't cause too much of an issue in the grand scheme of things.

All of these tactics are a must for waking up slow campaigns and getting some much-needed momentum going for your series.

3. Keep Creating More Ads and Writing More Books

I may sound a little bit like a broken record here, but it's always helpful to have a reminder of what you should keep doing. Amazon ads are an every-week commitment, and you should continue to research keywords and grow your number of ads over time.

Meanwhile, it's also essential to keep adding to your catalogue of books. This strategy fits in extremely well with running ads and doing quarterly discounts. For example, you could set up 40 Amazon ad campaigns in the month of June, run a discount promo for your series in the month of July, and then release a new book in the month of August. If you keep up this strategy for an entire year, then you're likely to see slow and steady growth each and every quarter. Plus, it gives you a lot more control over whether or not your income increases over time.

Nonfiction author James Dillehay, who we first mentioned in Chapter 1, was determined to make ads work for him. When the ads didn't serve nearly as fast as he'd hoped, he began playing around with his campaign end dates and budgets. His tweaks helped his ads to gather more impressions and clicks, which increased his royalties in turn. But these small changes led to much bigger results down the line.

As he continued to gather more data, he found that some of his books deserved more attention than others. He renewed his focus on his most profitable titles, and after 18 months of diving deep on the ads he reached his first five-figure month. Sometimes, the small changes can help you get enough data to make the bigger (and much more profitable) ones in the future.

It's easy to blame Amazon ads or just say that they're "random" and only work occasionally. I hope that by showing you have more control over the ads than you think, you'll put these necessary quarterly actions into your calendar.

* * *

Chapter 11 Exercises

1. Of the budget and date tweaking methods we mentioned above, which do you think you'll consider trying first when your ads are one month old?

2. Have you ever run $0.99 or free discount promotions before? If not, there are hundreds of blog posts out there on this tried and true subject.

Visit our Links Glossary at BestPageForward.net/Ads for Kindlepreneur's top promo sites.

3. What are some of the ways you've kept yourself writing despite a busy schedule in the past? Which strategy would you like to employ to keep writing and advertising at the same time?

4. How will you stay patient with this slow and steady marketing strategy over the next 3-12 months?

* * *

There were times over the previous nine months where I wasn't sure if Erin would follow through. When authors are resistant to trying some of the strategies we share, they often find themselves at a standstill. And while Erin had many challenging moments during our time working together, the final three months of our coaching time were incredible.

Erin barreled forward with the techniques at hand. She pushed herself to write two additional romance novels and ran regular discount promotions on her series starters. Erin kept her 5-10 ad creation habit up each and every week. And the results spoke for themselves.

When we first started working together, her sales had slumped below $100 a month. As our last sessions drew near, she had her best launch ever and a $2,500 royalty month. I was extremely proud, but it wasn't about her hitting some number. It was all about the hard work she'd been willing to engage in the entire 11.5 months we'd worked together.

Her voice was a little quiet during some early meeting small talk. "I'm not exactly sure how you did this."

I smiled. "I didn't do anything. You did all the work, and you should be really proud of yourself."

"Does shocked count as proud?" she asked. "I can't believe this is the second to last session."

"Time flies when a short man you won a prize from forces you to do book marketing," I said.

Erin blinked her eyes a few times before rubbing them with the corner of her sleeve.

"You'd think I'd be relieved that this twisted game is almost over," she said. "Now, I'm terrified I won't know what to do next."

"You already know what to do. Keep writing. Keep advertising. And keep watching your royalties versus your ad spend."

She sniffled. "Right. Not too complicated. But maybe you could just tell me step-by-step every little thing I need to do for the next five years."

I really was going to miss her. "What? And spoil the fun?" I asked with a laugh. "I can't tell the future, but I'm happy to give my best guess of what you should expect going forward."

CHAPTER 12

WHAT SHOULD I EXPECT WITH AMAZON ADS IN THE FUTURE?

I've always been impressed with authors who've been able to keep up advertising for months at a time. It can't be helped when life intervenes and occasional issues crop up. But to maintain the hard work for weeks, months, and quarters at a time takes discipline and clear, defined goals.

Like Erin dragging her feet on making changes, most of the authors I've worked with are at least somewhat stuck in their ways. But the folks who pushed past that initial fear and got into the routine of advertising, writing, and promoting typically saw positive movement. And a handful, like Erin, combined their skill with a little bit of luck to get some stellar financial results.

And within an hour, I'd see how this impressive author would fly on her own.

"So," I said. "What do you want to talk about today?"

"Too many things," she replied. "Maybe you can just remind me that I'm not going to crash and burn as soon as we take the training wheels off?"

"You didn't find success because I spent the last year whispering in your ear. It's because you figured out how to do the work and make it your own. Eventually, you might've even gotten there without me."

She leaned forward. "While I appreciate you being polite, I think I would've made three ads with $1 bids, lost two-hundred bucks, and given up on the whole thing without your help. So, what do I do now?"

"TikTok, Pinterest, and Instagram. All at the same time," I said with an almost-straight face. "I kid. I kid."

She laughed. "Been there, done that. Seriously though. I think I know the answer, but—"

"Of course you do. Over the last six months, your royalties have gone up over ten times." I was so proud of her for accomplishing such an impressive feat. "We always think there's this point at which we have to 'change it up,' but there's nothing wrong with continuing to do what works. I've said it before, but if it ain't broke, don't fix it. Remember?"

"Right. Five to ten ads per week, quarterly promos, and keep writing new books to market. I guess I just thought you had to do it all. Like if you couldn't spin all the plates at once, you were a failure."

"I've been there," I said. "I'm still there from time to time. But if I was going to follow my own advice it would be to double, triple, and quadruple down on whatever's working."

She nodded. "Simple enough. Thank you."

While I was used to Erin's sarcasm and snarky humor, I couldn't help but feel surprised at her warm and genuine gratitude. I took another mental snapshot to save the moment for a rainy day.

"You're welcome," I said.

She was silent for a long moment before speaking again. "You know, there's only one thing I regret in all of this."

"What's that?" I asked.

"I just wish I could've gotten a little more out of the sci-fi." She sighed in disappointment. "I'm enjoying the new take on the romance, but it's a shame that it'll have to sit on the back burner for a while."

"Not necessarily," I said.

She frowned at my latest curve ball. "I thought you said I should double down on what's profitable."

"I got you a little parting gift," I said. "Something that might help you get the best of both worlds."

* * *

I'm extremely grateful to have been a part of many authors' success stories. Seeing some folks take these strategies and turn them into $1,000, $2,000, or $5,000+ per month has felt like a true blessing. But I'm also proud of the people who have made smaller gains, too. Any improvement is reason to celebrate.

It's my hope that the above story and my context below will help you to understand how you could potentially find strong results as well.

Let's recap what we learned and discuss what's next.

How would I describe the system of *Self-Publishing with Amazon Ads* in a nutshell?

- Step 1: Create 5-10 low-bid, relevant ads to your profitable series starters each week (with 39 cents for series starters, 34 cents for standalones, and 15 cents for children's or low content books)
- Step 2: Assess profitability and conversion rate after 100 clicks to each book
- Step 3: Keep running ads to the books or series that are profitable
- Step 4: Consider tweaking the sales pages of the books or series that aren't profitable

- Step 5: Each quarter, use coordinated discount promotions and wake up sleepy ads with budget and duration tweaking
- Step 6: Using profitability and market trends as a guide, continue to write books that give you the best chance of profit and creative fulfillment

Continuing to rinse and repeat this strategy over time can help you to cumulatively receive higher profit per month. It's a simple but difficult system to integrate, but once you've got it going, you can raise the ceiling of your self-publishing earning potential.

As we draw to a close with our tale and our time together, I think it's important to keep an accurate perspective on advertising. Amazon ads aren't about the quick wins and the big paydays. They're part of a greater strategy that may take months or quarters to realize.

These ads can help you determine if the books you have are profitable or not.

Greylin Reuss was an overworked EMT who wrote books on the side when she first encountered our Author Ad challenges. Applying many of the same concepts we've shared in this book, she saw her royalties begin to rise. Around the same time, she began writing to market, conducting the necessary research to get her subgenre just right for scores of hungry readers. With the combination of great books and low-bid ads, Greylin went from under $1,000 a month to her first six-figure year in less than 12 months' time.

Greylin is one of 10 authors we've documented who've eclipsed the five-figure a month mark. We've seen dozens of authors hit the high four-figures and hundreds reach that incredible $1,000 a month mark.

Sometimes, doing the proper steps in order with a method that seems counterintuitive and strange can produce incredible results.

If you have books that might be profitable with the right kind of marketing, then the system may help you see solid results in a matter of months.

Now, if you don't have a book that's profitable, Amazon ads still have a place for you. They serve as a litmus test for whether or not the book has a chance with some tweaks. Gathering 100 clicks initially and then an additional 100 clicks after changing a cover, blurb, subtitle, etc., may help you to turn around a struggling title or series.

If you have a mix of profitable and unprofitable series, then you can spend most of your time advertising the money maker and some of your time trying to rebrand and/or relaunch your less effective titles.

If you'd like a video walkthrough of some of these key concepts and the technical aspects of ads, then you may enjoy our free quarterly 5-Day Author Ad Profit Challenges. In addition to teaching advertising strategies, we offer consistent support and a welcoming community.

We currently run our challenges once per quarter in January, April, July, and October.

Want to get some additional advertising support as you embark on this journey?

Join us for our next upcoming class at AuthorsAdvertise.com!

There's no question, it'll be hard for you to reach the heights Erin achieved in a single year. But most things worth doing take time, energy, and willpower to complete.

I think you absolutely have what it takes to do it. You reading this book was an important step on your journey to get to where you want to be. Now that you know what to do next, it's time to turn these ideas into actions.

Thank you for buying and reading this book. My team and I look forward to seeing you around the fantastic author community.

* * *

Chapter 12 Exercises

1. What's the #1 thing you took away from this book?

2. Based on the strategy and tips within, what's your next step in advertising your books on Amazon?

3. What's your goal with Amazon Advertising over the next 6-12 months?

* * *

"Is this the part where you're going to pitch me on a time share or something?" Erin asked. "Or maybe a bridge in New Jersey?"

I shared my screen and brought up an image file I'd just received this morning. "Actually, I wanted to give you this."

On my screen was a cover I had commissioned for Erin's old sci-fi book with a brand new to-market book description and design. It was exactly what a reader might expect to see on the bestseller list.

"What on Earth is this?" Erin asked.

"I didn't want you to think I was totally against you writing sci-fi," I said. "I thought a fresh coat of paint might help you improve that conversion rate. And give you an extra shred of hope."

"What the F?" Erin didn't say F. "This is incredible. Thank you! But, I'm confused."

"When you've got a series that's working well enough but could be doing better, there's nothing wrong with trying to fix up the things that aren't quite there yet. Especially, if you really care about them."

"This must've cost you a fortu—wait," she said. "Your own team did this, didn't they?"

I nodded. "What can I say? Best Page Forward Plus does a great job."

Erin chuckled. "Uh-huh. Well, either way, this is amazing," she said. "You really did go above and beyond with this whole thing. I don't know how I would've done this without you."

"It really was a lot of fun," I said.

"You planning to do another contest?" she asked.

"Maybe," I said with a smile. "Possibly on email marketing."

"Wow, you never stop, do you?" she said. "You should listen more to that Zen Monkey of yours and take a break from working so hard."

I laughed. "It's a Zen Lemur. And you're probably right."

"Oh, I wanted to tell you. My husband is on the verge of getting a job," she said. "You really should feel some pride for helping keep us out of the poorhouse."

I did. I always did. And I always would.

"Erin, you're the one who did the hard work," I said. "And I have a feeling you're going to keep doing it."

"Stop being sweet, Guru!" She sniffled as she dabbed the corner of her eyes. "You're going to make me cry two calls in a row. But you really think I can keep all this up?"

"I *know* you can," I said with emphasis.

After the call ended, I sat in front of the laptop for a solid minute as I reflected. Nearly every author I'd met had put in the same number of hours as Erin to make themselves a better writer and a stronger marketer. But by focusing on a few key areas like profit, data, routine, and patience, she'd taken that effort and turned it into an incredible result.

There would be no shortage of tasks for her to do for the rest of her career to maintain and grow her sales. But for the first time in our entire year together, I didn't just hope she could do it. I knew she'd continue to succeed.

I let out a satisfying exhale as I brought up my calendar and list of tasks. There were more authors out there who needed a nudge toward more profit. I rolled my wrists, opened a blank document, and got back to work.

EPILOGUE

The next few months were pretty normal for me and the Author Ad School: more free classes, another 5-Day Author Ad Profit Challenge, and a whole lot of hard work. All the while, I continued to follow Erin's progress through the sales rank of her books and the occasional social media post. Each win I witnessed led to a mini celebration in my office. My joy doubled when I saw that her husband had started his new job while her books kept selling.

Isn't that the best of both worlds? I thought.

Later posts revealed that her romance releases continued to grow in popularity, and she even found success with a new series under her sci-fi pen name.

Despite my best efforts, I began checking on Erin less and less frequently as a new year-long coaching endeavor began. That's why it caught me completely by surprise when I received an email notifying me about a lengthy blog post called, "What I Really Think About Bryan Cohen."

Throughout back-to-back meetings with the teams at Author Ad School and Best Page Forward, I unsuccessfully forced myself not to think about the post that awaited me. Once my obligations ended, my fingers sprinted me over to Erin's post.

I braced myself for the worst and began reading.

"A lot of you have been asking me what it was like learning Amazon ads from Bryan Cohen. In fact, I get more messages about that than I do my fiction (step it up, readers). Let me start by saying that I was entirely skeptical at the beginning. I assumed that Bryan's whole thing was smoke and mirrors. I mean, low bids? Who'd believe *that* would ever work? He had to be all hype and marketing with no substance underneath, right?"

I could feel my heart thump a little louder in my chest.

"Even a few months into our time together, I wasn't sure. I wondered if all his woo-woo talk about patience and thinking about the future was giving him more time to fuel the getaway car. And right when I was thinking about giving up on the entire endeavor, my royalties and my profit went up. Can you believe it?"

I started breathing a little bit easier.

"Weirdly, it wasn't all about the money for him. Even though he has thousands of students, he made me a priority and genuinely seemed to care about me and my success. As much as I fought him along the way, if it hadn't been for him, I definitely would've ditched this process right before it worked. And now thanks to his teachings, I make over $5,000 a month on my books."

I thought about the state Erin was in when we had our first meeting. I hadn't known how dire her financial situation had been. She didn't know which books to promote and how to think about her backlist like a business. Now she was making over 50 times what she made in the 15 months prior. My smile grew wider.

"Maybe he'll always come off like a bit of a guru. But if it weren't for my guru, we would've lost our house. As frustrating as all of the tech stuff was, I'm glad I listened to the data. I'm glad I put in the work. And I'm glad I met Bryan."

My eyes scanned down to the final paragraph.

"Enough of this mushy stuff. I'm gonna go make 10 more Amazon ads and scrape the dog poop off the porch."

I shut my laptop and sat in silence, allowing myself to marinate in my feelings a little while longer. Her post reminded me about something one of my coaches said.

When folks choose not to study with you or hear whisperings and rumors that keep them away, you can tell yourself, "It's not their path."

The random chance of a contest had set Erin on a path with me. At first, it wasn't what she wanted. However, it ended up being exactly what she needed. I was overjoyed that it worked out for her.

As I basked in the gratitude for the opportunity to help Erin succeed, I started to wonder who would be next on the path of more profitable Amazon ads. I couldn't wait to meet them.

* * *

Want to get free videos and support to help you improve the profitability of your ads? Go to AuthorsAdvertise.com or scan the QR code to register and join our next free Challenge.

* * *

Would you rather get started right now and hop directly into the videos? You can take the Challenge any time of year AND get weekly live calls, lifetime support, and a whole lot more when you join Author Ad School.

Scan the QR code below and select Add to start learning the low bid, high profit system today!

ABOUT THE AUTHOR

Bryan Cohen is the CEO of Best Page Forward, an author copywriting agency that has written over 4,500 book descriptions for the author community. He's also an author who has sold 140,000+ copies of his novels and nonfiction. Each quarter, he runs the 5-Day Author Ad Profit Challenge, an event that helps authors create more profitable ads. He lives with his wife, daughter, and cat in sunny North Carolina.

Go to www.AuthorsAdvertise.com to join our next free Author Ad Profit Challenge!

THANK YOU FROM BRYAN

Thank you to everyone who helped make this project a reality. And thanks especially to the amazing backers who supported this project on Kickstarter. You are the reason I began this project, and your support is what saw me through to the end.

A.C. Dawn

A.E. King

Ali Winters

AMTWriting77.com

Andrew Einspruch

Anita Soelver

Ann Schauperl

Anna Taylor Sweringen

Annie Beth Donahue

Anmarie Uber

April M. Cox

Arnoldo Rosas

Arthur Steckel

Arya Matthews

Audrey Hughey

Author Kandy Ostrosky

Barry A. Lehman

Beatrice Stewart

Beau Spearman

Beck Grey

Berta Platas

Bethany Kelly

Blaine Moore

Bonita Guti

Brenda D. Williams

Brenda Gayle

C.K. Johnson

Cathy Peper

Charlene Perry

Charlotte O'Shay, Romance Author

Chas Williamson Books, LLC

Christopher Chan

Christy Piper, author of 'Girl, You Deserve More'

Craig A. Price Jr.

D. Anne Paris

Daniel MacLagan

Daniele Jennings

Dave Baxter

David Anson

David Gatward

David Sharp

David Singer

Deborah Wallace

Devin Cowick & Don Wilson

Devin Joubert

Diane Lewis

Dineen Miller

DJGainer

Don A. Carey

Dr. Fred Capps

Dr. Rita Garcia

Dr. Sandra Tanner

E.D. Hackett

E.V. Bancroft

Edale Lane

Edward T Duranty

Eleanor

Elizabeth Meyette

Emma Luna

Eric H. Brown

Eric J. Gates

Erica Reeder

Francesco Tehrani

Frédéric Lippold

G.K. Brady

Genie Hermoso

Geoff Keall, Author of The Semantics of i AM

Ginger Chambers

Gracie Bond

Harley Christensen

Hayson

Hazzum Productions

Hiram Patterson

J.C. Fields

J.S. Jaeger

Jace Killan

Jaime Samms

Jake Evanoff

James Husum

James Michael Starr

Jamie Davis

Jamie L. Saloff

Jane Cannon, Reed Shore Press

Jean Jacobsen

Jeanine Hansen

Jeffrey L. Gurian

Jeffrey Mason

Jen Lassalle

Jennifer Rose

Jerry Evanoff

Jesikah Sundin

Jim Fortune

Joanna A. McKethan

Joanna Schilling

Joanne Jaytanie

John McGuire

Julian Hilton

K. C. Herbel

Kai Strand

Karen Stillwagon

Kari Bovee

Katherine Caron katherinecaron.com

Kathleen A Osborne

Kathryn

Kathy Downs

Kathy Manos Penn

Keith Hedger

Kim Ann, author

Kimberly Amato

Kimberly Anne

Kristal Hollis

Laurie Harrison

Lee Dunning

Leslie Lindsey Davis

Libby Fischer Hellmann

Lily J. Adams

Linda Ganzini

Linda Karimo

Linnea Dayton, publisher, Dayton Publishing LLC

Lisa Barry (aka Gargoyle Girl)

Lisa Tapp

Lizabeth Scott

Luca Storm

Malcolm Coon

Mandi Lynn

Manuel Ruiz

Marilyn Peake

Marina Reznor, Author

Mark Gregory Probert

Marlene Jenkins Cooper

Mary Lou Dickinson

Marylee MacDonald

Matt DiMaio

Matthea W. Ross

Max J Miller

Meg Stewart

Mel Erickson

Mel Walker

Melanie Snow, Paranormal Cozy Mysteries

Michael Axe

Michael J. Allen

Michael Price Nelson

Michelle Kidd

Mikael Monnier

Mike Cisneros

Mike O'Neill

Miri Stone

MK Clark

Monica Leonelle

Nadine Galinsky Feldman

Nancy Gardner, author of Dream Stalker

Nancy Paulson Fox

Natasha #1

Nathan Stockwell

Nicole Richard

Niki Palmer

Paris Woods

Patrick J. O'Connor

Patrick O'Donnell

Peg Lewis

Peter Szczensny

PJ Peterson

R. Lawson

Randy Thurman

Raven Oak

Rebecca Loach

Regina Felty

Rhonda Lane

Rhondi Salsitz

Rita Goldner

Rob Baddorf

Robin Florence

Roland Denzel

Ron Vitale

Rosemary O'Brien

S. J. Pajonas

S.J. Pierce

Sara Cate

Savannah Jezowski

Scarlett & Ron Moss

Shauna L. Perez

Shea Patrick

Sherile Reilly

Shu Ying

Simon Goodson

Stacy McKitrick

Stephanie Kreml

Steve Mastroianni

Steve Wolfson

Sue Paterson

Susan Cork

Susan Laspe

Susan Lower

Suzanne de Planque

Sylvia Melena, Founder & CEO, Melena Consulting Group

Tanya Hales

Tasche Laine

Taylor Crawford

Teresa Mills

Thomas Umstattd Jr.

Three Muses Ink

Tom Acquin

Tracy Fredrychowski

Valerie J. Brooks

Velvet Vaughn

Victoria Tait

Vijay Kumar Maru

Village Drummer Fiction

Wanda Landis

Wolf Pack Entertainment

www.Bardstone.com

Yelena Ten

And many more who preferred to remain anonymous.

* * *

Go to www.AuthorsAdvertise.com or scan the QR code below to join our next Author Ad Profit Challenge!

Printed in Great Britain
by Amazon